Cover photo:

Temple of the Inscriptions, Palenque, Mexico
(where I learned about the Mayan Calendar in 2010)

It's Not The Same Friday

A story of personal change

Jeannie Benjamin

Copyright © 2014 Jeannie Benjamin
All rights reserved.

ISBN-13: 978-1493712472

To Dylan and Charlotte

for all your Fridays
.....and the days in between

CONTENTS

Acknowledgements

Preface   1

PART ONE 1964-1991:   CHANGE HAPPENS   3

Chapter 1   The day I met The Beatles   5
Chapter 2   We're all going on a summer holiday   11
Chapter 3   A change of plan   17
Chapter 4   A pivotal year   25
Chapter 5   Pushing the boundaries   31
Chapter 6   Discovering my power   37
Chapter 7   The years following 1983   41
Chapter 8   A fatal car crash   47
Chapter 9   My mother speaks to me   53

PART TWO 1987-1997:   CHANGING THE WORLD   65

Chapter 10   Achieving a few ambitions   67
Chapter 11   Standing for Parliament   73
Chapter 12   An even greater ambition   79
Chapter 13   Pursuing my goal   83
Chapter 14   The years spent chasing a winnable seat   87

PART THREE 1993-2012:   CHANGING MYSELF   97

Chapter 15	What did I really want?	99
Chapter 16	My father speaks to me	107
Chapter 17	Learning to love myself	119
Chapter 18	It's amazing what a visit to Thailand can do for life	125
Chapter 19	My father speaks to me again	135
Chapter 20	Another change of direction and a visit to my father	145
Chapter 21	I can do it!	151
Chapter 22	From Parliamentary Candidate to Porridge Queen	161
Chapter 23	Another unexpected change of direction	167
Chapter 24	The path of change continues	177
Chapter 25	A final message from my father	181

Afterword   189

A Postscript   191

ACKNOWLEDGEMENTS

I am grateful to Dom Leo Maidlow Davis, Head Master of Downside School, for permission to quote from "Downside By and Large", by Dom Hubert Van Zeller, published by Sheed and Ward, (1953).

I gratefully acknowledge the usefulness of the quotations from the following songs: "A Day In the Life" by The Beatles, "Summer Holiday" by Cliff Richard, "Nobody Told Me" by John Lennon, "Coming Around Again" by Carly Simon, "The Times They Are A-Changing" by Bob Dylan, and "Beautiful Boy" by John Lennon.

I am also grateful to the following people, alive or dead, for their wisdom and insight: Andrew Marvell, Heraclitus, The Buddha, Sarah Barry, Mark Twain, Margaret Mead, Anthony Robbins, Dame Rennie Fritchie, Thich Nhat Hanh, Susan Jeffers, Harold Macmillan, Helen Dunmore, Karl Marx, Leo Tolstoy, Robert Burns, Aldous Huxley, Wayne Dyer, Ari Badaines, Louise L. Hay, Mahatma Gandhi, Dr. Patricia Crane, Elisabeth Kübler-Ross, Julia Cameron, Jimmy Buffett, Dr. Seuss, Lewis Carroll, Victor Hugo, Pericles, Reinhold Niebuhr and to my friend Gill Gardner for the proof-reading and general feedback.

I acknowledge with enormous gratitude my debt to my mother, Margaret Elizabeth (Betty) Benjamin and my father, Eric Arthur Benjamin, whose fortitude and strength of character provided me with such a strong foundation to my life.

Finally, I would like to express my thanks and appreciation to my partner, Martyn Lavender, for his patience and forbearance in listening to my endless mutterings about "my book" ever since I have known him.

"Oh Damn, I've been hit. I'm going down. Number two take over, number two take over……"

Preface

"You could not step twice into the same river; for fresh waters are ever flowing in upon you."
Heraclitus.

Towards the end of the 1970s Friday afternoon meant coming home to Crunchie Bars, Turkish Delight and comics. I was married, my two children were at junior school and I was working as a teacher in a primary school. There was a very special feeling about those Fridays: a cosiness, a warmth, a feeling of anticipation and excitement. The end of the school week had arrived and the weekend stretched ahead, full of promise and relaxation, - no stress, no homework until Sunday, and time for the children to play games, to read and to watch television.

As soon as we all came home from school we dropped our bags, rushed around to the sweetshop-cum-newsagent which was only fifty yards away and bought our favourite sweets and comics. Then we scurried back to sit around the kitchen table in the basement of our four-storey Victorian house near the Vine Cricket Ground in Sevenoaks, Kent, to enjoy our rewards for getting through the week and arriving at Friday. Bliss!

It wasn't until some years later that my daughter reminded me of a brief conversation that we had had on one of those celebratory Fridays. She recalled that there had been some general discussion about how glad we were that Friday had come around again and I apparently said to her: "Ah, but it's not the *same* Friday."

How outstandingly obvious that is, but how very salutary. Many of us in our nine-to-five jobs say as we approach the end of the working week, "Thank goodness it's Friday"; there was even a chain of restaurants, a television programme, a pop song and a film all with a similar name. It is generally acknowledged that Friday is a special day, that it is always something to look forward to. However, we forget that it's not the *same* Friday which keeps coming around, like Groundhog Day or the horse on a fairground carousel. On the contrary, each Friday takes us a week further into our lives, while we go on thinking "It's Friday again."

But it isn't Friday *again*; it's another Friday, a different Friday, a Friday on which we become a week older than we were on the previous Friday. Each new Friday that arrives takes us to a new place in our lives and we forget this at our peril. Those Turkish Delight and Crunchie Bar-filled Fridays of the late 1970s would lead me and my family into many new and different places throughout 1980s, the 1990s and into the third Millennium.

Before (and long after) I made that comment to my daughter I was acutely aware of two lines in a poem by Andrew Marvell:

"But at my back I always hear
Time's winged chariot hurrying near"

Indeed it was my ever-present awareness of that thought which finally tipped me into writing this memoir. At the age of sixty-two and becoming ever more conscious of my own mortality, I found I had an urgent need to start "getting it all down on paper". This may not be an unusual response to getting older; nevertheless I hope that others may be able to relate to some of my reflections on my personal experiences. I have enjoyed the process of recalling them and it has helped me to feel that perhaps my life might not have been lived in vain.

PART ONE
1964-1991

CHANGE HAPPENS

"Everything changes. Nothing stays the same. Make your peace with that and all will be well."

The Buddha

"Nothing good lasts and nothing bad lasts."

Sarah Barry
(my maternal grandmother)

Chapter 1

The day I met The Beatles

"I read the news today, oh boy"
from "A Day in the Life", by the Beatles

"Mum, John Lennon's been shot!"

    I was in the bathroom on the third floor of our large Victorian home in Dartford Road, Sevenoaks, on the morning of Tuesday December 9th, 1980. It was nearly 7.30am and I was getting ready to go to the school in nearby Edenbridge where I was teaching. I was startled to hear my teenage son's voice calling down from his bedroom on the top floor. I pulled open the bathroom door shouting back "What do you mean?" I couldn't comprehend it. "He's dead," was my son's reply. I raced upstairs to the radio in his bedroom to hear the news coverage. I was in tears. Surely this couldn't be true. (I am writing this on the day when celebrations are being held to mark what would have been John Lennon's seventieth birthday and I still feel sad when I think about his sudden death.)

    I went to school in a daze. I had to get there early that day as I was due to arrange a display of teddy bears in the school hall ready for the morning assembly. I couldn't think about anything besides the tragic news and couldn't understand how everyone else was talking about normal things. The headteacher and my other colleagues mentioned John Lennon's murder in passing but the news had not affected them in the way that it had affected me. There were many people who felt a connection with John Lennon even though they did not know him personally, hence the huge outpouring of grief both in this country and all over the world, but there was an added reason why I felt so especially touched and it was because my son knew this that he had called to me so urgently that morning. I had told my son and daughter many times the story about how, many years earlier, I had fleetingly met John Lennon and this story had gone down in the family annals.

It was 1964; I was twenty years old and in the final year of my Teacher Training Course at Digby Stuart College, Roehampton. I had a boyfriend with whom I had been "going steady" since the age of fourteen and we were part of a group of friends who used to meet regularly in the coffee bars of Richmond and Twickenham. One of those coffee bars was called "Open City" where we sat around tables fashioned in the shape of coffins, our legs dangling down into a trench, supposedly below the earth. It was a dark place and we considered ourselves very bohemian. In short it was a typical sixties scene. One day, over a cup of frothy coffee, an idea cropped up between us which, as we discussed it further, gradually materialised into an actual plan. My boyfriend, Chris and his friend Tim decided to buy an old red London double-decker bus and we would take it on a holiday abroad with a few friends. The idea of course owed something to the fact that the film "Summer Holiday", starring Cliff Richard, had appeared on cinema screens in the previous year, but we always denied that this had had any influence on us! In February the boys went ahead and bought a bus for £450 from Hounslow garage. It was an RTL 1950 model (Registration No. LLU 829) which was the immediate precursor to the famous Routemaster. Chris and Tim duly got their special Public Service Vehicle Licence and we prepared to put our holiday plan into action. We would advertise for other young people to come and join us (for a fee); we would obtain advertising to cover much of the cost and it would be my job to research possible routes.

We had not got very far with our preparations when Tim received a phone call from Twickenham Film Studios, which was just around the corner from his house. The Beatles had just begun shooting their first film "A Hard Day's Night" at those studios; the director had spotted our bus parked in the (rather large) back yard of Tim's house and he asked whether he could hire it for a day for use in the Beatles' film! A flurry of phone calls ensued between us that evening as we tried to catch our breath! This was at the beginning of Beatlemania; only three weeks earlier the Beatles had returned from taking America by storm on the Ed Sullivan Show during their first visit to New York, and now the Fab Four were coming round to us on the following day! It seemed unbelievable then and it seems even more unbelievable now. We knew there would be tight security and we imagined that they would be ushered into Tim's house while preparations were made for shooting the scene. I had visions of myself serving them coffee (that's what girlfriends did in the sixties) while they sat patiently in Tim's front room. It wasn't quite like that however.

On Tuesday March 10th, 1964 I took the day off college and arrived in good time to make the coffee. The bus was already in position on the other side of the road when the Beatles arrived in a large black saloon car. And there they stayed. My hopes of waiting on them with cups of coffee were dwindling fast. I was disappointed. I spent most of the day sitting on the flight of stone steps which led up to Tim's house, watching retake after retake of the bus pulling away from the fake traffic lights which had been placed in the road for the scene, while the Beatles sat in the saloon car behind. After a couple of hours I had a better view of them as they were all suddenly ushered out of the car and up the stairs of the bus on to the top deck. The director made sure that all of us onlookers remained on the other side of the road well away from the cameras but my eyes were fixed on those four famous young men at every single moment. Then it happened. One of the film crew approached Tim's mother and asked if John Lennon could use the toilet in her house. This was my chance! John began to cross the road, accompanied by Wilfrid Brambell, who played Paul McCartney's fictional grandfather in the film, and who was well known as the old man in the popular TV programme "Steptoe and Son". They had both been "taken short"! As they crossed the road towards me and approached the front door my heart skipped a beat! They both passed within inches of me as they walked quickly through the open front door of Tim's house, along the hallway and into the toilet which was on the ground floor on the left hand side. I was surprised that the two of them went in there together (although it was quite a large toilet)! I waited in the hall patiently; I had a plan and my heart was beating fast. As the toilet door opened I stepped forward in front of them, barring their way.

"Hello John," I said boldly. "Would you and Paul and George and Ringo do something for me? Please would you write your names all over the inside of the bus?" And I handed him a few large felt-tipped pens which as a trainee teacher I had ready in my coat pocket. I explained that I had the authority to ask him to do this since the person driving the bus was a friend of mine. John looked somewhat surprised but readily agreed. I cannot remember his exact words in reply as I was so overawed by the fact that I was actually speaking to John Lennon and as I handed him the felt pens our hands actually touched! Wilfrid Brambell stood behind him looking a bit bemused. Taking the pens, John walked back across the road to the bus and ran up the stairs to re-join the others on the top deck. I watched him handing out the pens to Paul, George and Ringo, pointing down at me and presumably explaining what I had asked him to do. They went about their task with gusto! I saw them leaping around and appearing to have great fun as they scrawled their names (and as I discovered afterwards a few quirky drawings for good measure) over the ceiling and walls of the top deck of our bus. It was an amazing sight! The filming of "A Hard Day's Night" then resumed and the rest of the day passed in a blur as far as I was concerned. I had met John Lennon! I had spoken to him and he had spoken to me! Our hands had touched! It had really happened! He had always been my favourite Beatle, the one I admired the most. Out of their early hits the one I had always loved was "I wanna hold your hand", and I had just touched John Lennon's hand! (In later years it became a family joke that this had happened just after he had had a pee!) That evening I went home and phoned all my friends, saying "Guess what, - today I met the Beatles!"

The following day I went around to Twickenham Studios and asked for my felt pens back! The Beatles weren't there but someone went into a back room and retrieved the pens for me. I've no idea what I did with them afterwards! Looking at the Beatles' autographs scrawled all over the top deck of the bus, I was reassured that it hadn't all been a dream. It was true. We arranged to preserve them by having them covered in pieces of Perspex. We didn't want anyone to rub them off!

After the bus had achieved this fame it was used later that year in another film, "Ballad in Blue", which was the life story of Ray Charles. This time I was a little closer to the action. There was a short scene in which a couple of children were filmed getting on the bus in London and while the scene was being shot I was sitting on the top deck with my boyfriend Chris. The filming took most of the night and I remember coming home at 4.00am, which was the latest I had ever stayed up.

The sad sequel to the story of the bus and the Beatles is that the scene that I watched them filming was never used in "A Hard Day's Night". We were given five complimentary tickets to the press showing of the film at Leicester Square on Monday July 6th, 1964 and we had to be there at 10.30 in the morning. I felt very honoured to be there but I hardly noticed what the film was about as I was too busy scanning the screen from top to bottom and side to side to catch the shots of our bus. I was so disappointed to find that there was no sign of it. It had ended up on the cutting room floor. A whole day spent filming and nothing to show for it; I could hardly hold back my tears as I came out of the cinema. I had been in the privileged position of being at the first ever showing of the first Beatles' film and my reaction was one of deep disappointment. It wasn't until I watched the film again at a later date that I appreciated it for the fun and zany picture that it was. I felt some degree of satisfaction when I saw the bus appear in the Ray Charles film but this was a small consolation prize and did not compensate for my bitter disappointment at there being not even a fleeting glimpse of our bus in "A Hard Day's Night".

Chapter 2

We're all going on a summer holiday

"We've seen it in the movies, now let's see if it's true" from "Summer Holiday", by Cliff Richard

After the amazing and unexpected Beatles experience we calmed down and resumed preparations for our original purpose in buying the bus: taking it abroad for our summer holiday. As part of our preparations we made a few day trips in this country as practice runs, taking groups of friends on outings to Coventry, Anglesey, Brighton and Goodwood. Singing along to guitars as we rumbled along the roads of England, with some of us sitting halfway up the stairs, we certainly felt as though we were actors in our own film. On the return journey from the motor racing at Goodwood the bus broke down and while the engine was being attended to by some of the boys, I decided that it would be fun to do a bit of dancing. I placed my transistor radio on the grass verge and began jiving with a friend while passing motorists looked on in surprise. Our fun was suddenly brought to a halt when a policeman drew up and told us that we were causing a hazard. I was about to answer back in a defiant teenage way when Tim restrained me. The policeman told me that he had just come from the morgue and wasn't going to take any nonsense. I felt duly chastened. Many years later that policeman's reference to the morgue, spoken on a Sussex roadside, was to come back and haunt me.

The bus having proved its mettle on its practice runs we set about preparing for our "Summer Holiday" experience. Wanting to make sure that we could afford our trip we placed an advertisement in "The Times" to recruit more passengers, specifying the age range. We sifted through the applications, invited the successful ones for interview and in the end chose thirty-five young people to accompany us at a cost of £28 each. We hired a room over a local pub called "The Rising Sun" (co-incidentally very similar to the title of a hit song of the time by the Animals) and we convened a meeting where we all got to know each other and sorted out the practical details. The bus was then given a revamp. Unlike the bus in the film "Summer Holiday", it was not fitted out like a caravan. There would be no kitchen area or bedrooms. With such a large number of people there would not have been enough space to put beds inside the bus; instead we would use it as a base for a camping holiday. We set to work stripping out most of the seats from the lower deck so that we could use it as storage space for all our camping equipment and the upper deck seats would stay in place to be used for seating while travelling. Everyone organised themselves into small groups and each group would be responsible for providing their own tents, cooking equipment and food. We would take three weeks to travel through five countries in Europe: France, Belgium, Holland, Germany and Switzerland. My sister Sally, who was an art school student, had the job of painting the flags of the five countries to fit the destination panels on the front of the bus.

It was my job to plan the itinerary. The route had to be very carefully researched because of the height of the bus; we didn't want to bump into any low bridges. I wrote to all the camping sites in advance to find out whether the terrain was suitable and to make sure there would be enough space for such a large vehicle and about fifteen tents. I was also the advance scout and navigator as I always enjoyed anything to do with maps and I had an "A" level in French. It was my job to sit at the front of the top deck and look out for obstacles; we had fitted an intercom between the driver's cab and the front seat of the top deck so that I could give a warning to the driver. There was one other aspect to this whole venture which gave it an even more surreal "Summer Holiday" connection. My boyfriend Chris, one of the two co-drivers of the bus, was acknowledged by all who met him to be a dead-ringer for Cliff

Richard. He had often been stopped in the street and asked for his autograph even before we had thought of organising this trip!

On Saturday July 25th, 1964 the forty of us, some of us local friends, others young people from various parts of the country who barely knew one another, gathered together in Twickenham, piled all the camping gear into the lower deck of the bus, climbed the stairs to the top deck and set off for our three-week adventure, waving from the windows and accompanied for the first few hundred yards by a camera crew from "British Movietone News". Our bus at last had its moment of fame on the silver screen as our departure was shown not only in the local newspaper but also in the newsreels on cinema screens in the following week.

It was certainly a unique experience. In some respects it could be viewed as a "rite of passage" as we all made our own personal discoveries along the way, coping with the jealousies and sexual tensions which were an inevitable consequence of such a large number of young people thrown together for three weeks. My mother's worst fear was that the bus would tip over and we would all end up in a ditch in a foreign field. However, apart from having a window smashed near Lille, Twickenham's twin town (where incidentally we were given a civic reception by the mayor) and getting stuck across a narrow one-way street in Belgium as we tried to turn around after going the wrong way, there were no major mishaps. I saw a black cat cross our path near Dunkirk and at the time I thought this was a sign of good luck but I learned later that it can also mean the reverse! Of course wherever we went there was much interest in the Beatles' signatures on the top deck. It became known as "The Beatle Bus" and a number of distorted stories went around the European press, including one headline which proclaimed that we had actually bought the bus from the Beatles! This headline was above a photo showing the bus in front of the Arc de Triomphe, which we had been obliged to drive around several times as the press photographers snapped away. Much to my mother's relief we eventually returned safe and sound on Sunday August 16th, 1964, the day before my twenty-first birthday. At my birthday celebration a few days later I had tears in my eyes as my mother placed on top of my birthday cake a little model of our wonderful bus.

I have told this tale of the bus and the Beatles many times over during the forty-eight intervening years and each time I am asked "What happened to the bus? It must have been worth a fortune with the Beatles' signatures and drawings on it!" Unfortunately I lost track of its whereabouts during subsequent years. Chris and his friend Tim went their separate ways the following year, with Chris selling his share of the ownership.

Me climbing into the cab of our bus in front of the Eiffel Tower August 1964

I do know that Tim offered the bus for sale later that year for the sum of £3,000 and was offered £1,300 from an American and £37 and 10 shillings from a Warrington boys' club! Both offers were refused and Tim used the bus for a couple of subsequent continental trips. I have learned that it was also used in the 1967 film "To Sir, with Love", starring Lulu, (sheer co-incidence that the registration number of the bus was LLU!) and that at some stage the top of the bus was cut off. I have no knowledge of what happened to the Beatles' signatures. The only objective proof I have that the Beatles really did sign their names on the bus is in a film clip from "British Movietone News" which can be found on the Internet.

It seems that in the early nineties the bus was refitted, given a new roof and restored externally and internally; apparently it now resides in a Transport Museum in Lowestoft. However it will always remain for me a very special and wonderful vehicle which gave me a unique experience. It will epitomise the swinging sixties in a way that few others will be able to claim.

Chapter 3
A Change of Plan

**"Nobody told me there'd be days like these,
- strange days indeed"
from "Nobody Told Me", by John Lennon**

I did not marry my bus-driving, Cliff Richard look-a-like, boyfriend. I had been going out with him for seven years since the age of fourteen; all my friends had expected us to get married, as we ourselves did. A year after the bus holiday he and I decided to emigrate to Australia on the "£10 pom" scheme. This was an assisted passage arrangement to encourage well-qualified people to live in Australia. My boyfriend was an architect's assistant and had accepted the offer of a job out there and I was a recently qualified teacher, so we would both be very acceptable to the Australian government. I went for my interview at Australia House in the spring of 1965 and when I was asked why I wanted to go and live in Australia I told them that I didn't see any reason why the mere fact of being born in a particular country meant that you had to live there for the rest of your life. This seemed to satisfy them and Chris and I made our plans. He would travel out ahead of me and I would join him a few months later. On Thursday September 30th his parents, his sister and I waved him off at Heathrow and I came home in floods of tears. He phoned me that evening from Switzerland where he was changing planes and we both marvelled at the short length of time it had taken him to get there compared with the three weeks our bus had taken in the previous year! I cried all night in the bedroom I shared with my sister.

Six weeks after Chris left I met the man I would marry just three months later. It was, as they say, "a whirlwind courtship".

He was a friend of my cousin David, who encouraged me to go out with this man because he had never liked Chris! I did and we fell in love. It was all very romantic. He would play his guitar and sing Bob Dylan songs to me; he would tell me wonderful stories as we sat in pubs and coffee bars, and we enjoyed visits to London's famous Carnaby street.

I spent that school term agonising over my choices. How could I let down my boyfriend of seven years by not joining him in Australia as arranged? But equally how could I abandon this man with whom I had just fallen in love? He asked me to marry him and I said yes. However, I had already given in my notice at the infant school in the London Borough of Hounslow where I was teaching and I was due to leave my job at Christmas. All my colleagues and all the children knew I was going to Australia to get married. On my leaving day there was a special assembly where I was presented with a small beauty case for my flight. I gave a speech of thanks, by then knowing in my heart that I would not actually be travelling to the other side of the world but unable to tell them that I wanted to stay in England and marry another man instead. I had to break the news to Chris that I would not be coming to Australia and was about to write to him when I discovered that his sister had got wind of my change of heart and had already written to tell him. His mother came round in tears to the flat where I lived with my mother and sister, understandably upset that I would be breaking her son's heart.

I have often thought that my decision to stay in England and marry someone else was based partly on an unacknowledged fear of travelling to such a faraway place to live. Not only was I intending to live in an unknown continent but the town where my boyfriend had secured a job was called Broken Hill, an isolated mining town in the far west outback of New South Wales. How could I, a feminist, have tolerated living among a bunch of unreconstructed males! I hadn't given this a thought. But falling in love with the man I had so recently met had given me the opportunity (the excuse?) to stay in England. None of these considerations was totally conscious but at some level I think I knew that there was some truth in them. Furthermore there was the added frisson of being in an exciting new relationship which had only a short projected time span. I was due to leave the country within a few months (although it has to be said I hadn't yet bought a ticket) and the prospect of never seeing this man again made the affair extremely romantic! There is nothing like forbidden fruit.

My mother was not at all happy at the thought of my marrying a man I hardly knew but she had been equally unhappy at the thought of my moving to live on the other side of the world. What made it even worse for her was the date I had chosen for my wedding. Because I was teaching (I had taken up a post as a supply teacher after leaving my permanent job at the end of the Christmas term) it made sense to get married and take our honeymoon during the half term holiday and so we chose Saturday February 19th for the wedding. I had not realised that this was the date on which my father had been killed. On the night of February 19th/20th 1945, at the age of twenty-five, my father, a Wing Commander and Master Bomber in the RAF, had been shot down as he led a bombing raid over Germany. I had never been particularly aware of the actual date of his death (in contrast to his birthday on June 27th which my mother always commemorated by placing a rose in front of his photograph on the mantelpiece). So in choosing this date to get married I was not being deliberately perverse; it was simply a convenient date and so on that day in 1966 my surname changed from Benjamin to Evans.

It would be an understatement to say that I did not have much experience of men. My father had been killed just a few months before the end of the war when I was eighteen months old and my sister Sally was only three weeks old. My mother was devastated by his death and we became her reason for living. I was brought up without a father, attended a single-sex convent school run by the Sisters of Mercy from the age of five until the age of seventeen (paid for by the RAF Benevolent Fund) and then went to a single-sex teacher-training college run by Sacred Heart nuns until the age of twenty-one. I had only ever had one boyfriend and had been going out with him for seven years. And yet I was totally sure that this man whom I had met only three months previously was the man I wanted to marry. Given my inexperience of men and the fact that my husband and I really didn't know each other very well before we plunged in, it is surprising that the marriage lasted as long as it did (twenty-one years). I had said goodbye to one man on Thursday September 30th, 1965 and on Thursday September 29th, 1966 I was giving birth to the son of another. I must have been pregnant on my wedding day but had not realised it at the time. What a year of change that was.

In the early years of the marriage there were only a few signs of the violence which later were to become more obvious and more frequent. Like most women in situations of domestic abuse I kept it quiet and pretended all was well, which for the most part it was. The day before our second wedding anniversary I gave birth to my second child, a daughter. We lived in an old house in the village of Frampton Cotterell, near Bristol, which my husband was restoring to make it habitable. His prowess in this field was remarkable, so much so that many years later he won a competition for which my mother had entered him and became the Daily Mail Ideal Home Man of the Year! No wonder that I never had any need to learn how to wield a paintbrush!

There are three occasions which stick out in my mind as early examples of my husband's violent behaviour. The first was when my son was only a couple of months old. We were visiting his mother and were sleeping downstairs in the living room with our son beside us in a carry cot. My husband made it clear that he wanted sex but I felt uncomfortable about it as our baby was next to us and my mother-in-law was sleeping upstairs in the room above us. I told him how I felt. He became very angry and aggressive and he forced himself upon me. I remember the look on his face which I can only describe as devilish. The next morning his mother came downstairs and said with a knowing look on her face that she had heard a lot of noise in the night; I remember thinking that she knew what had been going on but I said nothing.

The second occasion which I can remember occurred not behind closed doors but in public. It was a few months later and again we were on a short visit to his mother's house in Twickenham. We were in Woolworths when something happened to make him cross. I can't remember exactly what it was; all I know is that I was holding my son in my arms (and by that time I was already pregnant with my second child) when I was hit sharply across the shoulders and back. It came with such force and suddenness that I could hardly believe it. I was dimly aware that passers-by looked shocked as I walked swiftly towards the exit. The physical and emotional pain of the experience was made worse by the social embarrassment I felt.

The third occasion took place a few years later. In the early years of our marriage we had very little money and did not have a telephone. We had an arrangement with a neighbour who kindly let me pass on their phone number to my mother. She would ring their number every so often and they would come and fetch me so that I could speak to her. On Christmas Day, 1970 I went to take a call from my mother who told me in a hushed voice that Chris, the boyfriend who had gone to Australia five years earlier, had come over on a visit and had been to see her. He had asked where I was living and she had told him. She quickly realised that this was not a wise thing to do as she knew that my husband would be angry and she was ringing to warn me that Chris was likely to come and visit me on Boxing Day. I was terrified, not because of Chris but because of my husband; I knew he would be jealous (even though I had rejected Chris in favour of him) and so I decided to say nothing to him.

On Boxing Day I decided that the best strategy would be to leave the house to avoid any confrontation between the two men and so I suggested that we all go out for a walk to give the children an opportunity to try out their new toys. Our son was then aged four and our daughter nearly three and we had given them a tricycle and a pedal car for Christmas. We were helping the children along the pavement with their new transport and hadn't got very far from our house when a car came along the quiet country road, slowing down as it approached us and a man's face peered out from the window of the driver's seat. I recognised Chris at once. I looked away immediately, as though he were a complete stranger and I distracted my husband and children by keeping them focussed on the task of keeping their vehicles moving and we walked swiftly on. I will never know for certain whether Chris knew it was me or not, but my guess is that he did. My husband did not suspect a thing.

The violent consequence of this encounter occurred a few years later. I was visiting my mother with my husband and our children who were then aged around nine and seven. She and Fred, my stepfather, whom she had married after I had left home, had moved to a bungalow in Steyning, Sussex and each summer we used to take the children to spend a week there. The bungalow was not far from the sea and my mother took the children for many enjoyable days on Shoreham Beach, which they loved. We always called it a "Special Children's Holiday" so that they wouldn't feel we were offloading them! It also gave me and my husband some time together and we often took the opportunity to go to the theatre in London. On this occasion we were enjoying one of my mother's sumptuous lunches before leaving the children with her and going to spend the night in a hotel.

During the course of the meal, my mother said casually "Do you remember the time when Chris came over to England looking for you?" Then she realised what she had said in front of my husband and told me later that she could have bitten her tongue out. I had kept this secret for nearly five years and now it was out in the open. There was a frozen silence as my husband tried to comprehend. Then trying to swallow his anger he asked me about it and I told him as airily as I could about the walk on Boxing Day. Inwardly I was trembling as I knew he was bottling up his feelings until we had left. We wished the children a happy Special Children's Holiday and drove to the hotel. As soon as we were in our room he began to hit me, hard and long. This was the worst beating I had had up to then.

Despite these bouts of violence from my husband I tried to make the best of it. There were many times when he was kind and loving and he worked hard to make the homes that we lived in not just habitable but beautiful. I enjoyed bringing up my two preschool children and was out of the labour market for seven years. We had no washing machine and even no bathroom for a couple of years. With two lots of terry nappies to wash every day by hand (the children were only sixteen months apart), and trying to eke out the pennies, life was a bit of a struggle. I remember once going to the local shop with enough money to buy only cheese and frozen peas. My life-saver was the Open University. I felt I had to do something to keep my brain alive and once the children were in bed and all the chores were done each day I would study from nine o'clock until midnight each evening. Over the next few years I gained a B.A. in Educational Studies.

As my children grew up and I went back into teaching my life was not unhappy. By the 1970s we had moved to Kent and eventually settled in the house in Sevenoaks. Compared with the early years of the marriage we had become much more prosperous. The children were approaching their early teens and my life revolved around teaching, cooking, cleaning, shopping and the general "busy-ness" of what I considered to be "normal life" in the second half of the twentieth century. The fact that my husband's behaviour was becoming more and more unpredictable was something I tried to ignore or "smooth over" for the sake of my children. We all colluded in his unreasonableness and just got on with our lives. I had got married in a Catholic church and I really believed in "for better, for worse."

Then one day in 1982 I answered a knock at the front door to a teaching colleague who had come to ask whether I would like to join her on a demonstration at Greenham Common where there was a women's peace camp. Although the idea intrigued me I smoothed down my apron and said no, being very aware that my husband was within earshot. My response however was only partly due to the fact that I knew my husband wouldn't like me to go; it was also because I had a view of myself as "not being the sort of woman who did things like that". After all, I was a married woman with the responsibilities of a family, a home and a job. A lot of things were about to change in the following year of 1983.

Chapter 4

A Pivotal Year

"Twenty years from now you will be more disappointed by the things you didn't do than by the ones you did do. So throw off the bowlines. Sail away from the safe harbour. Catch the trade winds in your sails. Explore. Dream. Discover."
Mark Twain

Some years later I decided I wanted to become a Member of Parliament. This was not a long-cherished ambition from childhood, nor had I been brought up in a "political" household. However, I do have memories of my grandfather, Stephen Barry, sitting by the fire in his council house in Twickenham, declaring vehemently over and over again to me and my sister that "matter is indestructible". He ran a local petrol station as a business, had worked as a miner in South Wales and was an atheist and paid-up member of the Communist Party. This was a matter of great shame to my mother who, along with her sisters and brother, had all been sent to a Catholic boarding school, at the insistence, ironically, of my grandfather's mother!

My desire to become an MP stemmed not from any influence from my grandfather but from some life-changing events which happened in 1983. This was a pivotal year in my life. At that time I had been married for seventeen years, my children were aged sixteen and fifteen and I was doing a full-time job as a teacher of children with special educational needs. My life was kept busy with working and running the family home; I remember spending the weekends (after that brief Friday afternoon respite eating chocolate bars and reading comics with my children around the kitchen table) cooking meals, washing and ironing clothes, cleaning the house and preparing school work. I was aged thirty-nine and would become forty in August of that year. Only much later did that fact seem significant, when my son was reaching his fortieth year and was also involved in a major life-changing episode.

I was a member of the National Union of Teachers. I had been a member ever since I started teaching back in 1964 and all it had meant to me was that I paid a small subscription out of my salary each month as a kind of insurance policy should I ever need representation. I had never considered taking an active part in Union politics. But now I was about to take a first tentative step in that direction. The way I became involved will have a familiar ring to those who have ever been to a union meeting. I started attending meetings simply because they were held in the building where I worked; someone asked me to take the minutes and I agreed. I had no idea how to do this so I just scribbled down everything anyone said. Luckily I am a fast writer!

Gradually I became sucked into the world of agendas, matters arising, apologies and any other business. One day I decided I would try and be brave enough to stand up and actually speak at one of these meetings. They were always very small gatherings, with an average attendance of about fifteen people but it still required a tremendous amount of courage on my part to get up and address the assembled group of colleagues. My heart was pounding as I began to clear my throat and I forced the words out of my mouth. Whatever point I was making only took a minute or so but I was still shaking as I sat down afterwards. This was a milestone for me and in the ensuing months I became assistant secretary to the local branch (called a local association by the NUT) and was required to organise meetings, book outside speakers and arrange catering. I enjoyed this extra dimension to my life and found it rewarding.

A further step along the path of involvement came when my name was put forward as a delegate to the next NUT Annual Conference which took place at Easter. This in itself would have been a big enough step for me to take but there was an added dimension: for the first time ever the Conference was due to take place on the island of Jersey. There I was, actually considering the possibility of going abroad at Easter, on my own, leaving behind my family and my parental responsibilities - I didn't do things like that! It turned out that I did do things like that. I put the idea tentatively to my husband and although there was some tension and unease about the whole thing, he agreed. (I discovered on my return that in my absence he had entertained a Japanese woman at our home and this was probably why he made less fuss than I had expected.)

Thus I was soon on a plane flying to Jersey for the first of the many NUT Conferences I was to attend. And I loved it! This particular conference was a very controversial one because of the sexual politics involved in the choice of venue. Homosexuality was illegal in Jersey and the rank and file of union delegates were extremely angry that the Union's National Executive had chosen to hold that year's conference in a place where the laws were so illiberal that it was a criminal offence for certain people to express their sexuality. The politicking, sitting on the floor with a cheese roll at a packed lunch-time fringe meeting, the card votes, the staged walk-outs, always defying the NUT National Executive Committee, this was the stuff of union politics and this was for me! I even wondered whether I would ever be brave enough to actually speak at an NUT annual conference. I did actually achieve this ambition five years later but a lot of very choppy water would have to pass under the bridge before then.

1983 was also a General Election year. Amongst the West Kent delegation at Conference was the President of our Local Association, who had recently been selected as the Prospective Parliamentary Candidate for the Constituency of Sevenoaks, and the General Election was due to take place a couple of months later on June 9th. During the course of Conference he started talking to me about the Labour Party and asked if I would consider joining it. What!! Again I didn't do things like that. I was a respectable married woman with children, holding down a full-time job and with a house to run, albeit now also an active NUT member. But of course this was to be my year of change and I told him that I would think about it.

I returned from Conference full of enthusiasm. I had saved the many dozens of leaflets which had been handed to delegates at every session and at every fringe meeting and instead of throwing them away as most delegates did, I brought them all back home in plastic bags to relive the whole experience and show them to my family. My husband just shrugged and my children showed some interest but the person who appreciated them most was Fred, my mother's second husband, who was a firefighter and an active member of the Fire Brigades Union. He was impressed with my new-found involvement in the Trade Union Movement and was the only person in my immediate family environment who had any real conception of what I was talking about.

Soon after that NUT Conference I initiated a number of changes in my life, the consequences of which were far reaching, though I did not fully realise their significance at the time. A week after returning from Jersey I walked down the road to the local Labour Party "headquarters" in Holly Bush Lane. This was a wooden construction, a converted greengrocer's shop, somewhat dilapidated and known to members as the "Labour Party Hut". It took some courage for me to walk in, but as this was in the run up to the General Election and it was a fine Spring day, the door was open and enquiries were being encouraged; as a new prospective member I was given a warm welcome. I had now joined the Labour Party and was ready to "get involved", in more senses than I could have imagined.

It was also during this year that my greater involvement in NUT politics began. I attended the NUT's first women-only assertiveness-training course, which attracted a lot of attention within the Union. I found it hugely rewarding and subsequently wrote an article about it in the Union's magazine, "The Teacher". I had always felt very strongly about the place of women in the world and felt a huge affinity with the women's liberation movement of the previous decade (despite having a very strong self-image as wife and mother) and I soon began to immerse myself in the sexual politics of the NUT. Those were the days of the slogan, "A Woman's Place is in her Union" and on one occasion I attended a lobby of MPs at the House of Commons with a large cardboard version of that particular logo strapped to my back! I had now started out on a heady political path and was enjoying the journey. No longer was I just a wife, mother and teacher; I had found two other very satisfying roles, that of Labour Party member and active trade unionist; I was soon to find a role which was even more heady - that of community activist.

Chapter 5

Pushing the Boundaries

"Never doubt that a small group of thoughtful, committed citizens can change the world. Indeed, it is the only thing that ever has."
Margaret Mead

Many years later I would give talks to women's groups and trade union meetings, using my own experience as a starting point. I would often begin by saying:

"1983 was a critical year for me. I did three very significant things: I attended my first NUT Conference, I joined the Labour Party and I went on an assertiveness-training course." I would then pause and say "….and four years later I got divorced".

The connection was not lost on my (mostly female) audience and it would always make them laugh. However, there were many other reasons for the divorce, the main one being the physical and mental violence I suffered at the hand of my husband. I do not deny that those three events in 1983 were contributory factors, but they do not in any way excuse his violent and cruel behaviour. I was changing and the man I was married to simply did not like it; the only way he could respond was with anger, jealousy and mind games.

Many songs in the charts of 1983 have remained strong in my memory ever since, each one being clearly associated with the highs and lows of that unforgettable year. "Sweet Dreams" by the Eurythmics, "Karma Chameleon" by Culture Club, "Billie Jean" by Michael Jackson and in particular "Every Breath You Take" by The Police, each one still makes me catch my breath whenever it is played on the radio. Every time I hear those songs I am taken back to events in a particular week or month of that year.

In the months leading up to my fortieth birthday in the August of that year I took part in the General Election Campaign, supporting the local Labour Party Candidate for Sevenoaks (which was a staunch Tory constituency where the Labour Party always came third) and I loved every minute of it. I remember sitting in the back of our "battle bus" as all the campaign vehicles later became known. Ours took the shape of a rickety open-backed truck, where we sat on the floor and listened to our candidate shouting through his megaphone "Vote for me!" as we drove up Sevenoaks High Street and through the surrounding villages.

After the election was over and we had seen our candidate reach third place as expected, my political momentum was still on a roll and my energy was high. I took part in The People's March for Jobs in London, chanting "Maggie, Maggie, Maggie, out, out, out!" and singing "Burn it down, burn it down, burn it down!" as we passed the Ritz! But I wanted to do more, to make some changes, to make an impact on the world. I soon got my chance. The popular slogan of the previous decade, "The personal is political", had a certain twist as in my case the political became very personal indeed.

The council swimming baths in Sevenoaks were due to close down and the local independent school was offering to build a new pool in its grounds for use by the general public. However, their offer was not as generous as it sounded since the public would only have access to the pool on a couple of days a week. The rest of the week would be reserved for the privileged pupils at the school (where my son also had a free place as a result of the selective system operated by the Kent Education Authority). With my newly sharpened socialist instincts I viewed this as a very inequitable proposal and I brought up the issue at the next meeting of the local Labour Party where I was by then a regular attendee. We decided to take some action to try and get the pool built elsewhere so that the public could have access to it during the whole week, as was the case in most towns throughout the country.

When I say "we" decided to take some action it was less of a Labour Party "we" and more of a double act between me and the male branch secretary. We had, as Jane Austen might have said, "formed an attachment" during the General Election campaign, which soon developed into a full-blown love affair. My husband had been having an affair with a young nurse not much older than our daughter and I had found out about this during the previous year. (This was not the first of his affairs.) There were rows and tears and he told me he had given her up but during the Election campaign I discovered that the affair was still going on a year later. Rather than have a second bout of tears and rows I made the conscious (but probably unwise) decision to ignore his behaviour and enjoy the relationship that was developing between me and the branch secretary of the Labour Party. I was genuinely in love with him and it was a thrilling time; we both felt like teenagers. He was also unhappily married and we lived the next couple of months on a sea of politics, love and danger.

I learned a lot about local political activism during those weeks of 1983. I discovered that, according to the Local Government Act of 1972, there was a procedure by which local people could make changes in their particular area and the mechanism for doing this was called a local referendum. In order to get the local council to hold such a referendum the procedure was clear. It required local people to hold a public meeting and get ten people on the electoral register to stand up and call for the referendum. This would be put to the vote and if carried the council was then obliged to organise the referendum. This was a discovery which became the trigger for action.

The branch secretary and I began our campaign. I had a letter published in the "Sevenoaks Chronicle", the first of many over subsequent months, deploring the proposal to build a public swimming pool in the grounds of a private school with limited use for the public. Then with the backing of the Branch Labour Party we organised and advertised a public meeting at the local boys' secondary state school. We were amazed at the response. Literally hundreds of local people filled the hall and feelings were running very high that evening. The meeting was chaired by the clerk of the parish council and after various speakers had been invited to have their say, the ten people who had previously agreed to stand up and call for a local referendum (the branch secretary and I of course being the first) duly stood up and had their names recorded and checked for their electoral credentials. The amount of press interest was huge. To have a local referendum was a big deal and I had been instrumental in bringing it about.

The council was now obliged to start the procedure for holding a local referendum. It was their responsibility to produce the ballot papers and polling cards so that the people of Sevenoaks could vote yes or no on the question of whether there should be a public swimming pool built in the grounds of the local independent school. A date was set for the referendum and in the weeks leading up to it my lover and I went into overdrive in our campaign to persuade the electorate to "have their say". The local Labour Party hut was our campaign headquarters where we printed leaflets by the hundred. We spent the school holiday months of July and August printing and then delivering leaflets, week after week, to houses in every street in the town. I got very sore feet!

We did not want our campaign to be seen as negative, so rather than trying to persuade people to vote "no" to the idea of a pool in the grounds of the private school with limited availability we offered them the alternative idea of a pool in the grounds of the local boys' state school with no restrictions on availability. The name of this school was "Wildernesse" and it was situated at the opposite end of the town. We had the campaign slogan, "Say Yes to Wildernesse", printed on yellow T-shirts which we wore proudly as we tramped the streets delivering our leaflets during that long hot summer.

While I was totally focussed on the swimming pool campaign my husband was continuing to make repeated overnight visits to the nurses' home in Hastings as he carried on his affair. Meanwhile our son was smoking cannabis with his school friends in Knole Park and our daughter was hiding herself away in her bedroom as she studied for her "O" level GCE exams, trying to ignore everything that was going on. We had become a truly dysfunctional family.

The referendum duly took place in September and the upshot was that the new swimming pool was not built in the grounds of the local private school. This was a huge success for our campaign as well a source of great personal pride. The council decided not to build the pool at the state school either. Instead they opted for "neutral ground" and a couple of years later a brand new swimming pool rose up on a piece of land behind the local Tesco Supermarket. This was situated in the middle of Sevenoaks High Street, symbolically halfway between the two schools at either end of the town. My husband called it "a monument to our pain" but I didn't see it like that!

Soon after the referendum result my husband and I both decided to begin the challenge of trying to salvage the remains of our marriage and I ended my relationship with the local branch secretary of the Labour Party.

Chapter 6

Discovering my Power

"Personal power is the ability to take action"
Anthony Robbins

A significant person whom I had met in the spring of 1983 was Rennie Fritchie, who later became Dame Rennie Fritchie, Commissioner for Public Appointments and a leading and powerful national public figure. At that time she was the trainer on the first Assertiveness Training Course I attended, run by the National Union of Teachers, which was to start me on the road to self-discovery and the realisation of my own personal power.

As a newly paid up member of the Labour Party I firmly believed that the way to make any changes in society was to join forces with others in "solidarity", a word I still like very much, and to use that combined energy to get things done. (This was many years before the Blair mantra of "together we can achieve more than we can achieve alone" became current within the Labour Party.) I remember making this point very forcefully one morning on that training course, saying to Rennie Fritchie and the whole group that one individual on their own would be unlikely to make much impact on the world. Rennie looked at me thoughtfully and the next day she brought into the group a cutting from a short printed article called "The Man Who Planted Acorns". I still have that piece of paper. The article is called "Taking Stock – Being Fifty in the Eighties" and it was written by Charles Handy. It is a BBC publication and tells the imaginary story of a shepherd who before the First World War went out planting a hundred acorns each day in a barren landscape. This amounted to thirty thousand acorns a year. Over the years the landscape was transformed and by 1947 the region was alive with streams, crops and villages. It is a touching story and demonstrates beautifully the power of one individual to make a change in the world.

This powerful tale had a significant impact on me and it was this which had given me the impetus to start my swimming pool campaign and to begin other campaigns thereafter. Social change can indeed come about as a result of one individual's action as much as it can from group pressure. Where would we be without Nelson Mandela, Mahatma Gandhi, Jesus Christ, Rosa Parks or each of the Pankhursts? Much later in my life I would again return to the view that change can be brought about through individual action, but this would come after my foray into the heady world of Parliamentary politics.

Having flexed my muscles on the local referendum in Sevenoaks I then ventured into the slightly wider arena of change within the county, Kent County Council. During 1984 and 1985 I took on more and more roles as an activist within the NUT; I attained the positions of Equal Opportunities Officer and President of the Kent Division and eventually was elected on to the national Equal Opportunities Committee of the NUT. I initiated a piece of research into women's under-representation in senior positions in primary schools in West Kent, which subsequently developed into a wider survey covering the whole of Kent and was later published as a small booklet entitled "Top Jobs in Kent Schools". I was extremely proud of this. Its main finding, which came as no surprise, was that although the majority of teachers in primary schools were women, it was men who held the posts of heads and deputy heads. I organised a conference on the back of these findings which was attended by Kent's Chief Education Officer and which culminated in Kent County Council being persuaded to declare itself an Equal Opportunities Employer. Although this is now commonplace, in those days it was quite an achievement, especially within a Tory-controlled local authority. The council had resisted by alternating between two defences, saying either that they were already an Equal Opportunities Employer and did not need to declare it, or that they could not make the declaration just in case they weren't! Once they had made that declaration I was invited to sit on two working parties for Kent County Council which produced a job-share scheme and a career-break scheme. Again this was pretty avant-garde stuff for the times!

As a result of the publicity received by the announcement of these two schemes I was asked to appear on Meridian TV, the local television channel. I was collected from my house in a chauffeur-driven car and taken to the studios in Maidstone where I did a live interview on the six o'clock news. I am still amazed at my boldness in agreeing to my first ever television appearance going out live! (Going where angels fear to tread?) I was so proud of my achievement in bringing more equality of opportunity to Kent's teachers that I wanted to broadcast to the world! I was congratulated afterwards by NUT colleagues, not so much for my performance but for wearing a bright green dress which they told me was a good colour for television! This was to be the first of many occasions when after being interviewed on television I would be complimented on some aspect of my appearance rather than on the substance of my argument, which most people had forgotten by the following day. I would ask my friends "What did you think of what I said on television last night?" and they would reply "I can't remember what you said but your earrings were fabulous!" This was a salutary lesson on the power of the image.

One amusing incident which occurred following the publication of "Top Jobs in Kent Schools" would provide me with an anecdote for the many speeches I would give thereafter on the subject of equal opportunities. On Friday October 16th, 1987 the landscape of Southern England was suddenly and completely changed; the area was battered by hurricane winds and this subsequently became known as "The Great Storm". Sevenoaks became famous when six of the seven enormous oak trees which grew around the Vine Cricket Ground were completely uprooted overnight. Many jokes went around, renaming the town "Oneoak". I woke up to darkness on the morning of October 16th. No electricity, no lighting. I had been kept awake during the night by the enormous roar of the gales and looked out of the window to see trees sprawled all over the ground. I switched on the radio and tuned into Radio Kent. There were reports of roads being impassable and of the destruction of the famous oaks. I was due to work at a school in the Weald that morning and it was looking unlikely that I would be able to get there. The radio announcer said that many schools would be closed and asked for all "Headmasters" to phone in to say whether their school was affected. My hackles rose! Did he not know that Kent Education Authority was an Equal Opportunities Employer and that all heads were now to be known by the non-sexist title of "Headteacher"? I was on the phone to Radio Kent in a trice. I spoke to the producer of the news programme and told him that it was now the County's policy to refer to Headmasters and Headmistresses by the generic term of Headteacher. He apologised and said he would rectify the matter and pass on my comment to the programme's presenter. I switched the radio on again in time to hear the presenter saying, "We have just been phoned up by a Headmistress ......"! It takes a long time to change the habit of language.

Chapter 7

The years following 1983

"People have a hard time letting go of their suffering. Out of a fear of the unknown, they prefer suffering that is familiar."
Thich Nhat Hanh

"Every Breath You Take" was in the charts for many weeks in the early summer of 1983 and this became a kind of leitmotif for me in the following years. 1983 to 1987 were four long years of personal trouble, torment and anguish – for me, for my daughter and for my son, at the hands of my then husband. Violence, physical and emotional, punctuated each of those years and we all suffered during that time in our various ways. It was a time of fear, anxiety, indecision, doubt, unhappiness and many changes of mind on my part as I struggled to find a way out.

I had been brought up a Catholic, had got married in a Catholic church and although I was no longer practising the faith I still thought that divorce was completely out of the question. "For better, for worse", "what God hath joined together let no man put asunder", those beliefs were still there, embedded in my mind, and my feminist ideals were struggling hard against them.

The idea of loving myself did not occur to me at that time. The Christian doctrine of "Love thy neighbour as thyself" seemed to concentrate on the neighbour at the expense of the self. It was only much later in my life, when I was training to become a Louise Hay Teacher, that I learned what it means to truly love oneself. It isn't about being selfish at the expense of others. It means giving true value and respect to yourself, indeed as you would aspire to do to others. Many women however, in this culture and others, are expected to deny their own needs and are socialised to become "people-pleasers" instead.

At that time I was certainly ignoring my own needs as I struggled with notions of duty about "staying together for the sake of the children". I had grown up without a father and I didn't want to deprive my own children of their father. But there was also another thing holding me back and it wasn't duty, it was fear. I was afraid, afraid of the unknown. I had gone from living at home with my mother and sister at the age of twenty-two, straight into marriage, never having lived on my own. I had not even lived away from home during my teacher training as I had been a day student at Digby Stuart Teacher Training College in Roehampton, which was near enough to my home in Twickenham for me to commute. I could not imagine what it would be like to live by myself and however dreadful the situation in my marriage was, and it was truly dire during those last four years, for me it was still a case of "the devil you know". How could I live on my own, - without a man? I was now in my early forties and I could not imagine how I would cope. What about all the practical stuff? Who would service the car? How would I put up shelves, or fix the washing machine when it broke down? How could I manage without a man to depend on? And equally daunting was the thought of how I would go about starting divorce proceedings. These thoughts were so frightening that I let the fear hold me back for four long and painful years.

Many years later in my work as a Trade Union Official I would carry out a great deal of work on the issue of Domestic Violence/Abuse. One of the statistics I learned was that a woman suffers an average of thirty-five incidents of her partner's violence towards her before she seeks help from any outside source or reports it to the police. This fits very well with my own experience.

There was one occasion when in a fit of rage my husband ripped the telephone connection out of the wall while I was in the middle of a call to my mother. I started running out to a public call box to reassure her that I was all right when I saw a police car arriving at our house. My mother had been so worried about me that she had called 999 on my behalf. On returning to the house I could see that my husband's rage had subsided but nevertheless the two police officers advised me and my children, now in their mid-teens, to pack our bags and leave. This was not the only time that the police had been called to the house but it was the only occasion that I was actually persuaded to leave it. In a state of shock we got into the police car and were taken to a nearby "safe house", a guest house designated for the purpose of protecting vulnerable people. Around midnight, just as the children and I were trying to settle down for the night, I was called to the phone and told that my husband was on the line. The police had, unbelievably, given my husband the number! I spoke to him and I'm not sure whether he actually threatened to burn the house down or whether I just got the impression that he might in fact do that. In any case he was so persuasive that I agreed to return home that night. The house owner gave us a lift back to our home and as we sat silently in the car I looked at the bewildered faces of my children and I felt ashamed and sorry for the part I had played in causing them so much anguish. We were greeted by a much chastened man.

While every woman's case is different it is apparent that most women in a situation of domestic violence have been led by their partners towards a state of dependency, whether financial or emotional or both, which is very hard to break. For me it wasn't the financial considerations which were the most worrying. I was a teacher, a capable earner, and although my finances would certainly be affected by a divorce I would still be very able to provide for myself. My children were approaching adulthood and soon would not need much financial support (university grants still being available in those days). No it was not the economic reasons that kept me stuck; it was the fear of being truly on my own in the world, of having to manage my life without that one other person to rely on, which I had been used to for the whole of my adult life. I made a written list of the pros and cons of staying with my husband and another list of the pros and cons of getting a divorce. One word kept appearing in both lists; that word was fear.

So despite living with a man who constantly undermined me, a man who played interminable mind-games with me, who flew into violent outbursts of rage on the slightest pretext, who would strike me violently without warning and who kept me, my daughter and my son in a constant state of tension and anxiety with his unfathomable and unpredictable behaviour I chose to stay with him simply because I was too afraid to make the break and start a life on my own. I kept thinking, "If only I could make him change, then everything would be all right"! I was yet to learn that I could not change my husband, that he could only change if he wanted to (and he showed no sign of wanting to change) and that the only person I could change was myself.

My son and daughter chose their own ways of dealing with the situation, but that is their story. It was my daughter who, from the age of fifteen to nineteen, encouraged and supported me until finally I managed to break free from my husband's tyranny. During one of the many heart-to-heart conversations we had sitting in the spare room which was now my bedroom, she urged me to leave her father, saying things like "Mum, just think how great it will be: you will be able to eat cold baked beans straight out of the can in bed at three o'clock in the morning if you want to!" I shall always be both amazed by and grateful for, her advice, her wisdom and her maturity and at the same time I shall always be sorry she was ever in that position at such a crucial stage in her own development.

I still find it difficult to say exactly how it happened, how in the end I extracted myself from where I had seemed so firmly stuck. But somehow my husband and I eventually managed to come to an agreement that our marriage had irretrievably broken down and we started divorce proceedings. Despite all my fears there I was, on Thursday November 5th, 1987, having taken that truly enormous leap and moved out of the marital home, proudly holding a letter from my solicitor announcing the decree absolute. I was in my own house (a much smaller one) at the other end of town in a street with the wonderful name of "Greatness Road", with my cat and my car and I was feeling so happy I could burst! I had done it. I was free! Free to live my life how I wanted, free to be myself, free from fear, free to be a truly independent woman. I went out and bought a pizza, a bottle of red wine and a cassette tape of "Every Breath You Take"! I stood in the doorway of my tiny living room surveying my new home, with a glass of red wine in my hand, the smell of pizza wafting from my oven, the sound of Sting's voice in my ears and a tear of joy in my eye, heaving a huge sigh of relief and happiness.

Just prior to that momentous move there had been another General Election in the spring of 1987. I had campaigned in support of the new Labour Party candidate for Sevenoaks (this was another source of great anger for my husband who, one evening when I was out, had sprayed a whole bottle of my favourite perfume over all the clothes in my wardrobe and between the sheets of my bed). It was during that election campaign that the candidate suggested that I should stand as the parliamentary candidate for Sevenoaks constituency at the next election in four or five years' time. This remark sowed the seed and slowly I began to fantasise about the idea. However I had enough practical things to occupy me at the time, getting divorced, finding a new home, preparing my daughter for university (my son having already embarked on his university career) and generally facing the everyday challenges of getting my car serviced, managing my own finances and mowing the lawn. I had made a decision never to attempt any Do It Yourself jobs since my ex-husband had been something of an expert and had positively discouraged me from helping him. As a result I had felt disempowered in that area but since I was able to afford to pay for any jobs which needed doing, I decided to make that my new policy thereafter.

Living in my new home in Greatness Road for the next few years was a great pleasure for me. Having made the tremendous leap from misery and fear to peace and independence I was enjoying the thrill of knowing that I could choose to live my life the way I wanted and I could indeed eat baked beans in bed at three o'clock in the morning if I wanted to. I never did, but it was nice to know that I could! It was soon afterwards that I read Susan

Jeffers' famous book, "Feel the Fear and Do it Anyway". I read the whole book one Sunday afternoon and how it spoke to me! I had already felt the fear and I had done it anyway!

Chapter 8

A fatal car crash

"Events, dear boy, events"
Harold Macmillan

Most of the changes in people's lives happen imperceptibly, rolling along as an inevitable part of growing up and growing old. But of course there are other kinds of changes. There are changes which are brought about by our own deliberate actions and there are yet others which occur out of the blue as a result of "events, dear boy, events", as Harold Macmillan once said in response to a journalist when he was asked what can most easily steer a government off course.

On Friday November 8th, 1991, at the age of seventy-three, my mother was killed in a car crash. A week earlier, during my half-term holiday, she had driven up from the Sussex town of Steyning where she lived, to spend the day with me in Sevenoaks. We went out for lunch in Riverhead, a nearby village and we had a lovely day together. She was still grieving over the loss of her second husband Fred, who had died in April that year from cancer. This was of course the second time she had been widowed.

During the course of the day's conversation we spoke briefly about death and as we chatted over a cup of tea in my house in Greatness Road my mother mentioned that she was not afraid of dying when the time came. I told her that if there ever came a time when she couldn't look after herself she would always be welcome to come and live with me. She left my house at three o'clock in the afternoon because she didn't like driving in the dark. I stood at my front door and waved her off, watching her as she drove up the sloping road and turned right at the top to join the main road. That was the last time I saw her alive.

The following Thursday I had arranged to meet a previous boyfriend in the evening for a drink and was getting myself ready. He was a soldier in the British Army and was currently based at Woolwich. We had met on a walking holiday in the Yorkshire Dales in the summer of 1989, a year after my divorce and had enjoyed a two-year relationship punctuated by his time abroad in Dortmund. I had ended the relationship with him a few months earlier because I had met someone else. So it was just a meeting for old times' sake and to tidy up a few loose ends. My new partner, who was working as a researcher in the House of Commons, had taken my daughter there that evening to show her behind the scenes as she also had a great interest in politics.

I was expecting the soldier to call for me at my house and then we would go out for a drink at the local pub. As the evening wore on and there was no sign of him I began to wonder whether I had got the arrangements wrong. Then my phone rang. It wasn't him; it was my mother. She was phoning to tell me two things: that she was calling off an exhibition of Fred's lovely oil paintings as she could not bear to part with them and that she was going to change her will. She and Fred had made mirror wills, leaving everything to be divided three ways between me, my sister Sally and Fred's sister Phyllis; (Fred had no children of his own). My mother now wanted her estate to be divided in half between my sister and me. She knew that Phyllis, now in her late seventies and with no children of her own, was a rich woman and would have no need of a large sum of money. That being said, my mother still felt she needed to talk it over with me; she told me that some part of her could not dispel a nagging feeling of disloyalty towards Fred. During the course of our conversation she appeared to resolve the matter within herself and told me that she had made an appointment with her solicitor in Steyning for the following morning to sign the new will. She wanted to clear it with Phyllis first (although of course there was no legal necessity to do so) and was going to drive to see her in Storrington, a short distance away, before keeping the appointment with the solicitor. That was the last time I heard my mother's voice. How thankful I am that my soldier never turned up that evening or I would have missed her call. I found out later that he had been expecting me to confirm the arrangements prior to that evening and as I hadn't done so he thought I had decided against it.

The next day, after teaching a child with special needs at a school in Edenbridge, I drove home a little earlier than usual. It was Friday, the end of the working week and I was looking forward to seeing my son. He was then living and working in Argentina but was staying with me for a brief visit. He met me at the front door, saying that Granny had had an accident and the police had just been round to notify me. No details, no further information. I did not know at that stage whether it was a road accident or an accident at home. I vaguely thought she might have had a fall at home and hoped this was the case as a car accident might be much worse. In a state of shock and panic I began making phone calls, to the police station, to the hospitals in the Steyning area, to my sister, to my daughter at work, to my mother's two sisters and brother and to my partner. He told me later that my voice was almost unrecognisable as I moaned through the words. Eventually I discovered that my mother had been badly injured in a car crash and had been airlifted by helicopter to Chichester Hospital.

My daughter left her office in London, where she was working as a solicitor, to catch a train to Chichester. My son stayed at home by the phone. My partner drove me the sixty miles down the M23 and A27 and as we drove along the country roads approaching the hospital, he tried to calm me down by saying that we would probably find my mother sitting up in a hospital bed wondering what all the fuss was about. Somewhere deep down inside me I knew the reality would be very different.

On arrival at the hospital we walked swiftly towards the Accident and Emergency Department. As we went inside we passed a room with an open door where I glimpsed a woman sitting on a chair, leaning forward with her head in her hands, sobbing. I felt sorry for her for whatever tragedy had befallen her. We were shown into a room with half a dozen chairs where we were met by a man who had the job of receiving the families of accident victims and gently explaining to them what treatment was being given. He told us that my mother, my lively, energetic and joyful mother with the lovely memorable laugh and so much enthusiasm for living, was now in the operating theatre undergoing an operation to try and save her life. I pleaded with him through my tears to let me go in there and see her and he gently explained that it was not possible. He said that we could have the use of that private room as long as we wanted. My sister and her ex-husband then walked into the room together and I realised that she was the woman I had seen a few minutes earlier through that open door, sobbing. My daughter then came running down the hospital corridor in her smart work suit. While we all waited for news from the operating theatre my sister and I went in and out of the hospital doors comforting ourselves with too many cigarettes and having a feeble discussion about how we would care for our mother if she survived. I think we both knew the possibility was remote.

      After a few hours the kind man who had greeted us earlier appeared again and as he walked towards us I just said to him "I know." He didn't need to tell me. The next few hours passed with various formalities and the only thing I remember with any degree of clarity is agreeing to accompany someone to the mortuary to do an official identification of the body. My sister and my daughter had left by then. I walked along a very long corridor making small talk with this man, trying to sound as normal as possible as I got nearer to seeing my mother's dead body.

      I walked into the mortuary and someone told me that all I needed to do when I saw the body was just to give an indication that it was my mother. I approached a kind of bed at eye-level, on which was lying a person, probably a woman, who was covered mostly with a sheet. Her auburn hair had been pulled up into a sort of shower-cap and I could just see the hairline. She had tubes coming out of her nose and mouth and her face looked grey. Her arms were resting on top of the sheet and they looked quite plump. I took one look and for a brief moment was about to shake my head and say, no this wasn't her, they had made a mistake, this wasn't my mother, how could it be, and then I realised that it must be. Denial I suppose. I phoned my Auntie Winnie to tell her that her sister had died and she asked me whether my mother had been given the last rites. This hadn't occurred to me and I suddenly felt very guilty. My mother was a devout Catholic and she would certainly have wanted to receive this last Sacrament. Hoping it was not too late I quickly arranged for a priest to come. Bizarrely this meant my having to return to the mortuary to accompany the priest while he performed the Sacrament of Extreme Unction.

I was gently ushered away to an office to sign a few forms before leaving the hospital. Before setting out for home with my partner we were directed to the local police station to collect a few of my mother's possessions which had been in her car. I was shown into a room at the back, in the middle of which was a table. My mother's large straw shopping bag, which I recognised, with her handbag inside it, was sitting there on top of the table, looking like some sort of monument. It was a stark image, for which I was not prepared and I suddenly felt very angry at the police officers; they seemed so casual and matter-of-fact about it. There was a pile of old newspapers nearby which they told me had also been in her car; I suppose she had been intending to take them for recycling. These were also given back to me like so much booty. We duly took it all away and put it in our car for the one and a half hour journey back to Sevenoaks in the dark. I was hot, sweaty and wet all over during that car ride home. It was a very different Friday indeed.

Two days later I attended the annual Remembrance Day service at Sevenoaks war memorial opposite the Vine Cricket Ground. My son and my daughter accompanied me. We were commemorating the lives of both my parents, one so recently dead.

Chapter 9

My mother speaks to me

"As individuals, we are shaped by story from the time of our birth; we are formed by what we are told by our parents, our teachers, our intimates."
Helen Dunmore

The death of a parent is a milestone in each person's life. Having my mother die so suddenly, with no time for the preparation that might be expected when a parent is growing older, I felt not only bereaved but cheated. There had been no time to prepare, no time to say our goodbyes, no time to adjust to the prospect of death and separation. "It's not fair!" I wanted to shout. Now both my parents were gone. Both had died in violent and tragic circumstances. But they had not simply died, they had been killed, cut down before their time. When both parents are gone from your life there is a consciousness of having moved up to the next generation, knowing that you are next in line. Although my children could still look upwards to my generation, that was no longer an option for me. I was now technically an orphan, although of course this term is usually applied to young children, not to a woman in her forties.

I learned more details of my mother's last journey in the days following her death. After she had phoned me that Thursday evening to tell me of her plans to visit Phyllis the next morning before going to see her solicitor, I imagine she would have had a disturbed night because of her loyalty to Fred. On the morning of Friday November 8th, 1991, she got into her little Fiat Uno to drive to Storrington, five miles away. She had left her check suit jacket on the back of the chair by the telephone table in the hallway of her bungalow. In the fridge there were two cream cakes, which she must have bought earlier that morning, ready to entertain two elderly ladies to tea that afternoon. She always referred to them as her "old dears".

She arrived at Phyllis's home, a beautifully furnished flat above the newsagent's and tobacconist's shop which was run by Phyllis's brother, Sidney. Over a cup of coffee my mother explained to Phyllis that she was going to change her will in favour of me and Sally, that she was doing this to make the best provision for her daughters and hoped that Phyllis would not feel offended. Phyllis responded in the way my mother had hoped. She said that she completely understood my mother's desire to make sure her daughters would be financially secure in the future, that she had no problem at all with the will being changed and there was no bad feeling. (Phyllis herself assured Sally and me of this a few days later and said she would sign a document for the solicitor waiving her right to any claim on the will.) She saw my mother into her car and waved her off back to Steyning.

The surface of the A283 on that windy November morning was wet and strewn with leaves. Taking a bend on the road near the village of Washington where she had enjoyed a caravan holiday with me and Sally when we were children, while Fred came to visit us there (was she remembering this at the time I wonder?) my mother's car veered into the middle of the road, straight into the path of an HGV lorry. The Fiat was crushed and she was fatally injured. One of the firefighters who attended the scene along with the air ambulance crew knew my mother. He had been a friend of Fred's and had attended his funeral seven months previously. He gently asked my mother to lift her arms as he helped to remove her from the wreckage and although semi-conscious, she had been very compliant and had murmured a few words to him. I am glad she had a friend beside her. (I did not learn these details until a year later when Sally and I organised a sale of Fred's paintings in Steyning in aid of the Firefighters' Benevolent Fund and a charity for Street Children in South America which my mother supported.

It was then that this friend of Fred's told us the story of his part in the rescue of my mother from her car.)

On the day following the accident I drove down to my mother's bungalow by myself to meet the police for certain formalities. As I opened the front door the first thing that caught my eye was her check suit jacket draped over the chair in the hallway. I went to make myself a coffee and saw the cream cakes in the fridge. After the two police officers had left I began a preliminary search through the documents in my mother's bureau. I'm not sure whether I was looking for anything in particular, but I soon came across an envelope labelled "Jeannie and Sally". On opening it I began my first serious weeping. Inside the envelope were twelve small pages of blue Basildon Bond notepaper on which my mother had written her life story. It was in small handwriting and on both sides of the paper. It appeared that she did not write it all at one time but on two or three different occasions over the previous few years. The final page, headed "The Last Chapter", was in the form of a letter addressed to me and Sally, and which (since she refers to the pain of the last six months since Fred's death) was obviously written just one month before her death. In it she says to us: "I hope you won't have to read this for a few years yet!"

This is what I read on those little pieces of blue notepaper:

I was born in South Wales into poor circumstances. My father had to abandon his studies to be a mining engineer on the death of his father – leaving a widow with eight children. So he became a coal miner. He married my Baptist mother when he was twenty-six and she seventeen and a half, rather to the dismay of his mother and seven sisters – all staunch Catholics.

They were very hard times for my parents; one of my mother's classic stories was of the time when someone gave my father 2s.6d. to put a bet on a horse, and they spent the money on food instead, - an amazing loaf of bread, potatoes and meat, - not bad for twelve and a half pence! They awaited the race result with bated breath, - luckily the horse was unplaced! My brother and two sisters and I were somewhat undernourished, though Mam was very indignant when the doctor said I was suffering from malnutrition! My favourite meal was bread and cheese and cocoa – I hated "cooked" dinner!

My father became unemployed when the pit closed, and in 1926, the year of the General Strike, my forceful little paternal grandmother descended on us for a family conference. I have a vivid memory of us children being sent out to play. The outcome was, the house (such as it was) was sold up, my parents went to London in digs and my brother aged eleven, myself aged eight and my two sisters of six and four were all packed off to St Elizabeth House, Bullingham, Hereford, where we were promptly baptised as Catholics.

The nuns were very kind but oh, the homesickness; I have a vivid memory of my sisters and I sitting on a window seat watching for our mother coming to visit. (We were always a very close family despite our parents' frequent quarrels!) We didn't see our brother much, - girls and boys were very separate. I can still see the boys on one side of the church, the girls on the other. We took to Catholicism very well. Another memory is of sitting on a nun's knee and being taught to say "Sweet Infant Jesus, make me a good girl". I said this prayer for years! Not <u>all</u> sweetness at the convent though, - I remember seeing a girl walking around the quadrant with a sheet over her head; she'd wet her bed!

We were only there eighteen months – long enough to completely eradicate our Welsh accents – learned to say come <u>here</u> instead of come <u>year</u>. My paternal grandmother had found a job for my father as a petrol pump attendant in St Albans, although he knew nothing whatever about cars. So we came to digs in St Albans and to a little house in Fishpool, then obtained a council house and went to the Catholic school of Ss Alban and Stephen. We were late making our First Communions but it was a memorable day at "Maryland" where our teacher nuns lived.

However, father's job ended when his boss had to enter a lunatic asylum {not caused by my father's behaviour (joke!)} and a few strings were pulled to obtain a similar job for him at Twickenham. So, for a while, we only saw our father on his day off; he used to come home on his motor bike, always bringing us a bar of Toblerone! Why Toblerone I wonder? It was always an event, Dad coming home.

Eventually we obtained a council house in Twickenham and moved into 23 Mays Road when I was sixteen. Happy teenage years followed – despite parent quarrels – lots of friends in the Invicta Sports and Social Club. I worked as a cashier bookkeeper in a shoe shop in Kingston. Long hours – incredible to imagine now, 9-7o'clock, 9-8o'clock on Fridays and 9-9o'clock on Saturdays, usually 10pm by the time I'd done the figures. I cycled home for lunch too, and usually went to a dance after finishing work on Saturdays!

I met my handsome Sea Scout when I was nineteen, he eighteen. I can still remember my first sight of him striding along Teddington High St in his Sea Scout uniform, just back from camping, all tanned and scrubbed and fit. Courting walks in Bushey Park every evening, such simple pleasures – mild snogging in the sitting room, shared with two sisters doing the same. How did we manage to refrain from going the whole hog – simply wouldn't have dreamed of it (well, maybe a dream) even if the opportunity had presented itself. Which it did actually when we went on holiday together in 1937 or 8 to the Isle of Wight. We were given adjoining rooms and only used the one bed. Snuggled up together but positively no hanky panky. Where is the innocence of yesteryear? However did we manage it?

We "courted" for eighteen months – marriage seemed years away. Eric went to White Waltham for weekend flying lessons with the R.A.F. Volunteer Reserve in order to save money for this. But as it happened we married much sooner! The war changed everything. Eric was called up to the R.A.F. immediately with all the twenty year olds and sent to I.T.W. at Peterborough, became a sergeant straightaway. We married December 3rd 1939, - a week's honeymoon (period all the time) at Possingworth Park Hotel, Bournemouth. Awful stuffy hotel, full of OAPs. Can't *think why Eric chose the place. We were glad to get home to a nice party his Mum laid on.*

Then Eric went to Benson for officer training and off to Newton Notts as a pilot officer on Battles (prehistoric plane), crashed and badly burned his hands – then off to Torquay to the Palace Hotel – then a RAF hospital, for a few weeks. Back to Bobbington to be an instructor for a while, then posted to Scampton, Syerston and Waddington on ops. Off to France (I'm living at home) and back in June 1940 when France fell – just in time for his twenty-first birthday – local hero! Wonderful time. (Bit of a blank here!) I was still living at 23 Mays – longing for his leaves. Was called up and sent to work at N.P.L. but not for long – became pregnant! Full of excited anticipation and very well.

Eric, Mam and Dad took me to super hospital for RAF Officers' wives to have Jeannie – convalescent home for fortnight afterwards, then back to 23 Mays and wonderful welcome and fussing – hard to part with Eric, but leaves were wonderful. He found digs for me in Lincoln near the aerodrome and we lived a "normal" married life for a while. Took Jeannie in carry-cot to mess parties. Then we were somewhat dismayed to find I was pregnant again, but soon adjusted. Went back home when six months gone – Eric getting home often. Went off to West Middlesex Hospital in the snow on January 30th and produced my lovely Sally on 31st. Eric brought us home to 23 Mays ten days later for a very happy leave. He went back on the 18th February and was posted missing on the 19th.

Black, Black days and nights, hoping against hope that he was in enemy hands. All the family a wonderful support and grieving with me. What a comfort my babies were – life had to go on – a daily round of feeding and nappies. A year later confirmation of Eric's death. Had gradually accepted it already.

From then on my life was totally centred on two little girls – my pride and joy – and the years flew. First Communions, Confirmations, birthday parties, open days and sports days – always lovingly attended by "the family" – overwhelmingly so as recently admitted by Jeannie and Sally. "Other girls' parents came, but we had hordes of relatives!"

Then came the teen years and boyfriends (theirs and mine). Met Fred – and were good friends, then lovers. Jeannie married in 1966, Sally in 1967 and then Fred and me at long last in 1968 in the little Parish Church at Steyning – a new life in such a friendly little town. A busy life with lots of visitors – such happy days.

My happy granny days started in September 1966 with Dylan, Charlotte in February 1968, Toby in January 1972 and a wonderful little late arrival, Rebecca in December 1979, "year of the child". Have had enormous pleasure from them all, and my two loving daughters, and am having a very happy old age! All this, and Heaven too?!!

The Last Chapter

To Jeannie and Sally,

Don't be sad when you read this, dears. Tears will be unavoidable but eventually the sadness <u>will</u> ease and memories will become happy.

I have survived six months without my dear Fred – six awful months, nearly drowned in tears and longing, and the inevitable regrets but I must repeat Fred's words – I, too, have had a wonderful life, so much joy and love and now I am trying to accept the inevitable sadness.

I am having so much support from you both, and all the family, and this wonderful community. I am so thankful for the happy twenty-two years I had with Fred and I am sure the memories will become happy eventually, though they are a torment at the moment.

I hope you won't have to read this for a few years yet! Just be strong and remember how lucky I have been and it is a comfort to me to know that you will both benefit financially. Have as happy an old age as I have had – lots of holidays!

(The following pages were written and numbered separately, but enclosed with the story as a sort of appendix, I think.)

One of my most treasured memories is of the night of June 17th 1940 – the day France fell to the Germans.

I awoke about 11.30 to see my beloved husband of a few months, standing at my bedroom door – weary, dusty and with a sprained ankle, but full of joy at reaching home.

He had arrived back at his aerodrome at Nantes after an early bombing raid that morning, to find the squadron had left hastily in the face of advancing Germans – my photograph the only thing left hanging on a tent pole. He jumped into a plane – a fighter, though he was a bomber pilot, and flew the channel! He crossed London on the underground, mingling with home going workers and arrived at 23 Mays Rd, Teddington, about 11.30.

This sounds incredible, but I so vividly remember his description of the utter chaos in France and the long lines of pathetic refugees he saw from the air and the contrast of the utter ordinariness of suddenly being among the London commuters on the underground.

What a rapturous reunion we had that night – I hadn't expected to see him for ages – was afraid he would have been taken prisoner as so many were.

And the next morning he answered the door bell to receive a telegram telling me he was missing. How we laughed!

We had a wonderful leave, visiting family and friends – he was quite the hero of our little circle. He had such a happy twenty-first birthday party on June 27th, before re-joining his squadron.

He did many more bombing raids, including several on Berlin, and was filmed by Pathé newsreel talking after one of these, and calling it a "piece of cake". On one raid fifty planes were missing and he received the D.F.C. and bar, and reached the rank of Acting Wing Commander, but alas, his "lucky" number, 77777, didn't quite make it. He was killed on February 20th 1945.

There were only two planes missing on that raid, announced on the one o'clock news, and I thankfully carried on breast feeding our three-week old second daughter (the first one was eighteen months old). But the telegram came at two o'clock and this time it was for real!

Forty years since the telegram came and ended my happy carefree youth. My babies of three weeks and eighteen months now middle aged and my darling is still twenty-five – age did not weary him or the years condemn. (He did not grow fat either or lose his teeth.) The years that I wished away with such a fierce young grief have passed. I have been re-reading for the millionth time his happy and concerned young letters:

"My dear one,
It was lovely to hear you on the phone, sorry to hear about the bad raids"

"My dear one,
You must take care not to slip on the icy roads now your time is getting near"

"My dear one,
Shall be oc. night flying tonight so may not be able to receive your call"

"Did a trip last night and didn't get to bed till 5o'clock – hope to get a few days leave, but don't get too excited in case."

The letters never fail to bring him and the times vividly to mind:

"Went to the cinema – 1/- seats, tell Mum"
"Had bed and breakfast 7/6,"
"Petrol 1/3 a gallon"
"Batman allowance of 2/- per day"

So long ago but still like yesterday.

My mother with Sally and me after our father was posted missing

Spring 1945

My mother's funeral took place two weeks after the crash, on Friday, November 22nd. It was held at the Catholic church where Fred's funeral service had also been held in April of that year and where she and Fred had got married twenty-three years earlier in 1968. The turnout was amazing. The whole of Steyning seemed to be there, spilling out into the churchyard and the street. She had made a big impact on the local community with her work as a stand-in granny, her visits to the "old dears" in a nearby home and her regular churchgoing. She was buried in the same plot as Fred on the Sussex Downs at St Botolph's. It was a surreal experience to stand there watching her coffin being lowered into the grave where Fred's coffin had been lowered seven months earlier, while Sally and I had stood supporting her on either side.

An inquest was held at Horsham on January 29th, 1992 at which the coroner recorded a verdict of accidental death. I have always been convinced at some intuitive level that my mother died because she was still struggling with the thought that she was somehow betraying Fred by changing her will. She had been grieving heavily for him and I am sure that this thought had taken her mind off her driving. Ironically one of her mantras to Sally and me had been, "You must always have one hundred per cent concentration when you are driving".

The further irony of my mother being killed as she was on her way to change her will was given further emphasis by Phyllis's subsequent behaviour. Although she had been the last person to see my mother alive and knew precisely what my mother's last wishes had been, Phyllis decided to break the promise she had made and to reinstate her claim to a third of the inheritance. I believe that her behaviour was influenced by her brother Sidney. A protracted legal battle ensued. Over the course of the next few months Sally and I presented Phyllis with offers of a four-figure sum of money in return for her agreement to acknowledge our mother's wishes that everything should go to her daughters. Many letters went back and forth from our solicitor to Phyllis as she continued to haggle over the amount of money she would get. This legal wrangling was very harrowing, extremely distasteful to us and of course it was the last thing that my mother would have wanted. Eventually, after a very lengthy dispute, Phyllis finally agreed to accept a figure and a settlement was agreed. It did not feel like a triumph but at least it was over.

PART TWO
1987-1997

CHANGING THE WORLD

"Philosophers have sought to understand the world. The point, however, is to change it."

Karl Marx

Chapter 10

Achieving a few ambitions

"Everyone thinks of changing the world but no-one thinks of changing himself"
Leo Tolstoy

On Thursday April 9th, 1992, five months after my mother's death, I stood for Parliament, but it had been a long haul to get there after my divorce in 1987. Immediately after the General Election of 1987 I had been given some encouragement by that year's Parliamentary Candidate for the Constituency of Sevenoaks to consider putting myself forward for the next one but at that time I was too busy getting divorced, moving house and getting my new life in order to give it much thought. However, when all these things had been dealt with I was free to follow my interest in local and national politics without the stifling and restrictive manipulations of my (now ex-) husband.

At Easter 1988, not quite six months after getting divorced, I achieved the ambition I had begun to harbour five years earlier while attending my first NUT Conference in Jersey: I gave a speech at the NUT Annual Conference. It was held at Scarborough and I spoke on the subject of prejudice against Lesbians and Gays. There was strong feeling around this topic and a motion was to be put forward to strengthen union policy on lesbian and gay rights.

One evening after the main business of conference had finished for the day I attended a fringe meeting on this topic and found it riveting; speaker after speaker told of how they faced prejudice and homophobia on a daily basis wherever they lived and worked. I was very inspired by the passion in all of their speeches and when I left the meeting I went to the bar of my hotel for a drink to calm myself down before going to bed. When I entered the bar I saw a group of conference delegates enjoying themselves and having a bit of a sing-song. As I sipped my beer it became clear that the songs I was listening to were not harmless ditties; they contained a number of homophobic references, and even used the term "nancy boys". I was horrified. The contrast between that and the earlier part of the evening was glaring. I got up to leave in disgust, expressing my feelings to the woman behind the bar. Her reply was "Oh don't worry about it, they don't mean any harm"! I ran up the stairs to my room and in a state of shock and anger I wrote the whole episode down. If I was brave enough, I thought, I would use this story in a speech on the floor of conference the following day. I was going to dare to get up and speak to more people than I had ever faced in my life!

The next morning my resolve had not lessened. I put in a request to speak and I was chosen! I heard the president say "I call Jeannie Evans from West Kent" and my heart was beating fast as I approached the podium. It was a simple speech; all I did was relate the story of the previous evening, emphasizing my shock that teachers of all people, in charge of future generations, should display such intolerance and unthinking prejudice. I was astonished at the response I received. A huge amount of applause followed. I stepped down off the podium with my body shaking; my nervousness had caught up with me. The motion was put to the conference and was carried overwhelmingly. I had been instrumental in strengthening union policy on lesbian and gay rights and it felt all the more remarkable to me that this had taken place less than six months after escaping the restrictions of my marriage.

The following day it was time to return home. As delegates gathered on the platform at Scarborough railway station I was surprised to be approached by a young man who was not part of the West Kent delegation but a complete stranger to me. He said he wanted to congratulate me on my speech; he had been one of the singers in the bar that night and my speech had helped him to realise how unthinking he had been in taking part in the general ridicule of gay people. I was astounded to realise that my small story could have made such an impact. When I got home I learned with even more surprise that my sister's husband, working at home in his study, had heard my speech broadcast on BBC Radio Four!

A few months later, in September 1988, I was chosen by the local party to be their delegate to the Labour Party Conference in Blackpool. This was serious and exciting stuff, - the first time I had ever been to a Labour Party Conference. My next ambition began slowly to take shape; now that I had actually spoken at the NUT Annual Conference could I ever dare to make a speech to a future Annual Conference of the Labour Party?

I had by now made a name for myself within Sevenoaks through my local Labour Party activities and on a broader level within the NUT at County and National level, being a Teacher Representative on the Kent Education Committee as well as having been elected on to the NUT National Equal Opportunities Committee. In order to carry out all these duties the Kent Education Authority gave me a generous amount of time away from my day job as a teacher of children with special educational needs. The more involved I became in politics and the less time I spent in the classroom, the less far-fetched it also seemed to imagine myself sitting on the green benches of the House of Commons. It was around this time that the 300 Group and the "Women into Public Life" campaign were making their mark. The 300 Group was a pressure group established in 1980 as a national, apolitical, voluntary organisation to campaign for more women in Parliament, the European Parliament, Local Government and public life generally. It was these ideas that helped to spur me on with my burgeoning ambition.

Following that first Labour Party Conference in 1988 I began taking the whole idea more and more seriously. (It was then that I had read Susan Jeffers' "Feel the Fear and Do It Anyway".) I began to subscribe to "Tribune", the left-wing publication of the Party, and this kept me up with all the insider talk. I had subscribed to an earlier publication, "Labour Weekly" when I was still married. Each week as it dropped through the letter box on to the doormat it was snatched up by my husband whereupon he either tore it into pieces and stuffed in the drawers of my filing cabinet for me to discover later or he secretly saved it so that he could use it as wrapping paper for my Christmas presents. The outer layer of wrapping was always a beautifully coloured shiny piece of traditional wrapping paper but underneath was layer upon layer of pages from old copies of "Labour Weekly". He loved watching me tear up Labour Party literature as I opened my presents while I pretended not to notice what I was doing! Such was my collusion in his mind games. But that was now all in the past. "Tribune" was a more useful publication than "Labour Weekly" as it was used by Constituency Labour Parties to publish details of their timetables for selecting prospective parliamentary candidates and to invite applications for nominations.

    I began to apply myself to the task. I drew up my political CV, had a photograph taken by a professional photographer and decided to apply for seats which were not too far away but which were more likely to be winnable than Sevenoaks. As the possible date of the next General Election drew nearer I was invited to give speeches to branches in the neighbouring constituency of Dartford and a little further afield in Harlow. I spent one evening speeding back and forth through the Dartford Tunnel to present my pitch to two different branches on either side of the tunnel within the Dartford Constituency. After I had been told by one of these branches that I had not been successful in obtaining their nomination I rang them for feedback a few days later. The male branch secretary told me "Your costume was a little too severe"! I wondered how many men's applications had failed because their suits were too grey! For the Harlow nomination meeting I wore a dress but this didn't do the trick either.

    The first stage of my goal - that of actually getting selected as a prospective parliamentary candidate was achieved in the autumn of 1990. However, the constituency for which I was selected to stand was not a winnable seat but my own constituency,

Sevenoaks, the fourth safest Tory seat in the country! I had accepted that I wasn't going to become the next MP for Harlow or Dartford so I had decided to lower my sights and go all out for the prize of standing for Parliament in my own constituency. That became my all-consuming goal and I longed for it above all else. I was well-known in the area, I had proved that I could run a successful local campaign and I was liked by party members. To stand for Parliament, albeit in an unwinnable seat, was perhaps a more achievable goal than actually becoming an MP so I put all my efforts into attaining it. But it was not all plain sailing. Another party member, who was a councillor on Swanley Town Council in the northern part of the constituency, also had his eye on the prize. He put his application in and each of us did the rounds of all the branches gathering support and we each received a respectable number of nominations. Because of his experience as a local councillor I felt he had a better chance than I did and I was worried that party members would think that I lacked the necessary experience. The date of the selection meeting drew nearer and as I prepared my pitch and my answers to possible questions I was getting very anxious and nervous. Even though I knew there was no hope of actually overturning the long-standing conservative MP I wanted desperately to be the one chosen to get the chance to stand and fight in my own local constituency.

 A week before the selection meeting was due to take place at the Constituency Party Headquarters in Holly Bush Lane, where my final pitch would be made, I received a phone call at home. It was my rival for the candidacy on the other end of the line telling me he had decided to withdraw from the race. I was ecstatic! Trying to listen to him explaining his reasons: pressure of work, family commitments, (maybe he also thought I was the favourite and he didn't want the humiliation of losing) I could only think of one thing. I was definitely going to be the next Labour Party Prospective Parliamentary Candidate for Sevenoaks! Putting the phone down, I burst into tears of joy. My dream was about to become true. At the final selection meeting the following week, party members expressed a degree of disappointment that there was to be no contest after all, but they nevertheless put me through a fairly difficult series of questions before they finally gave me their seal of approval. I was now the official PPC for the constituency in which I lived.

Chapter 11

Standing for Parliament

**"I know nothing stays the same
But if you're willing to play the game
It's coming around again"
from "Coming Around Again", by Carly Simon**

The weeks and months between getting selected to stand for Parliament and the announcement of the date of the general election afford time for building a campaign, garnering support and preparing a strategy. I needed to appoint an agent and an offer came forward at the next meeting of the local party. He was working as a part-time researcher at the House of Commons and therefore was well placed to access information and I used this to the full. One of the MPs for whom my agent worked was Keith Vaz, who was kind enough to come to Sevenoaks to support me in a campaign that I was running to improve the local bus network. He spoke at a public meeting arranged by my agent and this provided some welcome publicity. He also spoke on a platform with me at a fringe meeting on transport at the next (1991) Labour Party Conference and even included my name in two Early Day Motions to Parliament. This was all very helpful for my public profile.

I was now utterly consumed with my candidacy. I was still employed by Kent County Council as a teacher of children with special educational needs; I was based in Sevenoaks and travelled to teach pupils in primary schools in the surrounding towns and villages of Riverhead, Edenbridge, Kemsing, Knockholt, Otford and Sevenoaks Weald, and I was also busy keeping my name alive in the local papers, attending meetings and carrying out interviews with local radio and TV. It was an advantage to be a teacher as I was often called for interviews not in my role as PPC (Prospective Parliamentary Candidate) but as an NUT representative, which gave me extra publicity. It was a hectic routine and for me it had a certain element of déjà vu about it. Eight years previously I had been running a campaign (about the swimming pool) with a man who was heavily involved in the local party and with whom I had been having a relationship. I was now in a relationship with my agent (having ended the one with the soldier) and here I was again, doing the same thing, running a campaign with a different man at my side. It may not have been the same Friday but it had uncannily similar resonances. I may not have repeated the pattern of my relationship with my violent husband but I seemed to be repeating a pattern of a different sort with these two men. The combination of sex and politics was a potent mix but I did not stop to dwell on this at the time and just carried on enjoying the heady rush of it all.

  There are a number of amusing stories to tell which occurred during the months of my candidacy. There was the time when I was on my way to do an early morning interview with Radio Kent in Maidstone in my little Renault 5 and it ran out of petrol. I pulled my car to the side of the road and was filling it up with petrol from the emergency can I carried in the boot when I heard a voice booming out from my car radio saying "we are expecting Jeannie Evans" (for I still had my married name at that time) "any minute now". Ten minutes later I was leaping up the stairs to the studio, arriving very much out of breath to carry out the interview!

  Then there was the time when I was called by the local television news to do an interview later that same day (I discovered that the media always want everything to happen immediately); they said they would come around to my house after school. There was no time to tidy the house let alone prepare what I wanted to say. When I got home the news crew was waiting at my front door, camera and boom mike at the ready, wanting to have the piece in the can for the six o'clock news. I hoped they would shoot the interview in front of the house, but they said they would prefer to do it in my back garden with the blue sky in the background. Thereupon I led them through my narrow terraced house, past the un-ironed heap of washing lying in the laundry basket, past the previous evening's unwashed pots and pans in the sink, and out into the tiny garden with its knee-high uncut grass, where I gave an interview on a subject which at the time must have seemed to me to be of great import, whatever it was.

It was about halfway between my getting selected as the PPC for Sevenoaks and actually standing in the 1992 General Election, that my mother was killed. One of my cousins, Philip, who was an active Labour Party member and a local councillor in Tandridge, Surrey, asked me at her funeral whether I still had the heart to continue with my candidacy. Without a flicker of hesitation I replied that I would certainly carry on and although I did refuse a few requests from the media for interviews in the weeks immediately following her death I gradually picked up the threads and carried on with my pre-election campaign. I was also at that time very busy dealing with the complications surrounding my mother's will. It is true that one way of coping with bereavement, although it may not be the best way, is to keep busy.

I have always felt sad that although my mother knew I had been selected she never saw me actually stand for Parliament. I sometimes wonder whether all my striving and all my achievements were at a subconscious level carried out in order to impress my mother and gain her love. I was never really convinced that she fully appreciated what a remarkable thing I was about to do. At the beginning of October, (a month before my mother died) my agent and I called on her unannounced at her bungalow in Steyning, on the way back home from the 1991 Conference in nearby Brighton. My Auntie Winnie and Uncle Aubrey were there on a visit; they had been going to see her more often in the months after Fred died. At Conference that afternoon I had been interviewed by the BBC during their live coverage, alongside Stephen Byers MP, on the subject of education. I was very proud of this and knew that my mother would have had the television on during the day because she knew I was there. I went rushing in to her kitchen saying excitedly, "Did you see me speaking on television this afternoon?" She replied, "No, I must have missed it when I went to make a cup of tea for Win and Aub!" I still find that memory disappointing.

On Wednesday March 11th, 1992, the General Election was called and I was up for it. I had been given four weeks' leave by my employer, Kent County Council; standing for Parliament was recognised as a public duty and as such deserved acknowledgment. From the moment the Election was called I stepped up from being a prospective candidate to becoming an actual Parliamentary Candidate. This was when it all got very serious. I was provided by the Labour Party with a huge dossier of material encompassing all the minutiae of Labour Party Policy. I was very conscientious and felt I had to study this as though I were about to sit an exam; that was certainly how I felt when sitting on a platform at a public meeting alongside candidates from the other parties and answering questions fired at us by the audience.

The four weeks of the campaign were a dizzy round of meetings, public appearances, media events and self-publicity. Despite Sevenoaks being a most unlikely seat to be won over to Labour, (such seats were known as "no-hopers") there was nevertheless a huge amount of work to be done. I set myself an achievable goal. I decided that my aim would be to increase both the actual number of Labour votes and the share of the vote in the Constituency so that on Election Day I would be able to feel some sense of satisfaction and my supporters would feel the fight had been worthwhile.

As at every General Election, the Labour Party nationally went into overdrive and the local party contributed its fair share of printed material. Large A3 size posters were produced, bearing my photograph and urging the electorate to "Vote for Jeannie Evans". Then came copies of my election address as well as stickers, leaflets, badges and posters in varying sizes, all emblazoned with my name in the familiar red and yellow party colours. Cardboard boxes full of all these items arrived day after day from the South East Regional Office and were stacked up high in the Labour Party hut in Holly Bush Lane, as well as covering a good deal of my living room carpet. The task of delivering the leaflets to the voters fell to a small band of willing helpers; many local members and supporters were being called away to put their effort into the more winnable seats of nearby Dartford and Gravesham. The party nationally felt it had a good chance of winning in this election; John Major was the Prime Minister and it looked as though he might be toppled. While I was fighting an unwinnable seat I took comfort from the fact that any sense of personal disappointment I might feel at losing in Sevenoaks would be compensated for by waking up on the morning of Friday April 10th, to find a Labour Government running the country. Of course this was not to be. It was somewhat ironic that I had my photograph taken standing in front of a huge roadside hoarding proclaiming the Labour Party's national slogan for this election, "It's time for change"!

Parliamentary Candidate for the Constituency of Sevenoaks
General Election 1992

At the end of it all I am pleased to say that I did achieve my objective. I increased the size of the Labour vote, receiving 9,470 votes from the people of Sevenoaks, for which I am grateful. I also put up the Labour share of the vote by three per cent and saved my deposit, despite warnings from the nay-sayers! I attained third place, after the Conservatives and the Liberal Democrats, which was the Labour Party's usual place. I hoped that local party members felt their efforts had all been worthwhile and that I had been a worthy candidate.

**Election Result
9,470 votes**

Standing as a Labour Parliamentary Candidate in a General Election, albeit in one of the safest Tory seats in the country, was a great honour and a privilege, and, it has to be said, one fantastic, enormous ego-trip for me! I loved it all: the sense of importance, the public renown, the feeling that somehow I was making a contribution, and not least shouting through a loud hailer: "Vote for me!" to the people in the streets of Sevenoaks and to the cows in the surrounding countryside. All of this was heady stuff for a woman who, just a few years earlier, had been too frightened to leave a man who was making her life a misery.

Chapter 12
An even greater ambition

"The times they are a-changing"
Bob Dylan

Following the 1992 election I resumed my former life as a teacher. I was once again an ordinary individual, leading a "normal" life. There were no more calls from the local media demanding my presence on a panel or at a studio interview; no more public meetings, speech-making or metaphorical tub-thumping. I was just plain ordinary Jeannie Evans going about her life anonymously, without any red and yellow stickers on her car, earning her living like any other member of the community. What a bump.

I had wanted so much to be the Parliamentary Candidate for Sevenoaks and I had achieved that aim. I had thought it would be enough to satisfy me. But I had tasted the fruit of a little bit of power and fame and now I wanted more. I had seen that simply by having a little bit of power in a community it was possible to bring about changes in people's lives and I could now see that the attainment of power at a higher level would mean that such changes could be possible in a wider arena. I decided that having earned my spurs by contesting an unwinnable seat I would actually have a go at the real thing. In other words I would pursue the goal of standing in a seat where the Labour Party had a reasonable chance of winning. My new ambition clarified itself: I wanted to become a Member of Parliament. I wanted to make changes in the world and at that time I still imagined that I could do this by sitting on those green benches in the House of Commons and helping to being about changes in the legislature.

So I made a plan. I would leave the teaching profession where I had spent all my working life; I would apply for other jobs in the public sector where my political and trade union experience would be an advantage; I would move to an area of the country where there were rather more winnable seats than in the South East. In short I would move north, stand in a safe seat and become a Member of Parliament!

Never having lived anywhere further north than Bristol this was a brave putative move. But there was nothing to keep me in the south of England other than a sense of familiarity. My children were now grown up and living away from home, my daughter working as a solicitor in the City and my son teaching in Argentina. I would be able to see them just as often from a home in the north of England as I could from my home in the south.

Leaving teaching would also be a very brave move. It was the only work I had ever known. I was comfortable with it. I had never imagined that I would ever do anything else in my professional life. At the Catholic Convent School in Twickenham where I was educated it was assumed that those of us who reached the sixth form would go into one of two professions, teaching or nursing, and that is indeed what we did. But it was thirty-two years since I had left school and I now had a new goal and a new sense of determination. I set about scouring the public appointments page in the Wednesday "Guardian" for likely jobs and my weekends were spent completing application forms and seeking references. Most of the posts I applied for were in the Trade Union Movement. I felt that with my wide experience as an activist within the NUT I would stand a good chance of finding such a post. I was hopeful that a job on the staff of a trade union would put me in a good position to get sponsored to fight for Labour in a winnable seat at the next general election in four or five years' time.

So the task was underway and my diligence knew no bounds. I succeeded in being called for a number of interviews over the following months, which spurred me on. I was very determined. An advertisement from NALGO (the National and Local Government Officers' Association) caught my eye. They were seeking applications for the newly created post of District Women's Officer. At their recent Annual Conference a resolution had been passed which obliged them to advertise this new post. There were actually twelve posts, - one in each of NALGO'S Districts throughout the UK. After my equal opportunities work in the NUT and my long-held passion for women's rights in the workplace I felt well qualified for the work as outlined in the job description and I applied for six out of the twelve posts, from Leeds to Reading. I could and would move anywhere.

After putting in my six applications I spent the month of August 1992 in South America, visiting my son in Buenos Aires and travelling from there to Tierra del Fuego, Santiago in Chile, and the Iguaçu Falls in Brazil. It was a wonderful experience. I was taking advantage of some of the money left to me by my mother, knowing that she would want me to do this. My then partner came with me (I would never have had the confidence at that stage to travel so far on my own) but since the General Election was over and he no longer had the role of my agent, the relationship was going off the boil and it was destined not to last much longer.

On my return home in September I opened three letters from NALGO inviting me for interviews. They were from the East Midlands, West Midlands and Southern Districts. Over the course of the next couple of months I attended those interviews which took place in Nottingham, Birmingham and Reading. I was successful in one of them; it was Reading. My hopes of moving north in order to find a safe seat thus received a small setback but my ultimate goal of becoming an MP remained firm. My final day in the teaching profession was Friday January 29th, 1993 and my first day working for a trade union was Monday February 1st, 1993. I had one weekend in which to prepare for my new life. The head of the Special Needs Unit where I had been working asked me what I was going to do on my first day at NALGO. "I have no idea!" I replied.

I drove the seventy-five miles along the M25 and M4 from Sevenoaks to Reading that Monday morning (for I had not yet found a new home in Reading) having no notion of what to expect from life in an office. The only workplaces I had known until then contained classrooms, corridors and playgrounds. It was exciting but also a little daunting to face the prospect of a future devoid of such familiar environments! I had a new job title, Women's Officer for the Southern District of NALGO and I was now a bona fide trade union official. My job description included encouraging more women to take an active part in the union, developing training courses for women and providing support in employment tribunal cases concerning sex discrimination, sexual harassment and equal pay. As in most areas of public life, it was men who assumed the leading roles in the union; they were the ones who became the branch secretaries, treasurers and negotiators and it was my task to persuade and inspire women members to take on these roles so that their power within the union was proportionate to their numbers. For me this job was so much more rewarding than teaching. I had found my metier.

A few months later, on July 1st 1993, NALGO merged with two other trade unions, COHSE (the Confederation of Health Service Employees) and NUPE (the National Union of Public Employees) to form the public service union UNISON. It was the largest trade union in the country and had over a million members, most of whom were women. Each of NALGO's former Districts became Regions and my job title now changed to Regional Women's Officer. A new era in my life was beginning.

Chapter 13

Pursuing my goal

"An archer cannot hit the bullseye if he doesn't know where the target is."
Anonymous

While thoroughly enjoying the challenge of my new life as a full-time trade union official I did not lose sight of my ultimate goal, that of getting selected to stand in a winnable seat and becoming a Member of Parliament. A couple of months after starting my job in Reading a by-election was called in the nearby constituency of Newbury. I decided to have a go at getting selected to stand as the Labour Party candidate. Although it was not a seat likely to be won by Labour and was therefore a diversion from my ultimate goal I thought it would raise my profile and look good on my CV to have been a candidate in a by-election. I would put up a good fight and people would remember my name. I duly got to work on updating my CV and seeking nominations from the local branches in Newbury.

While making the long journey from Sevenoaks to Reading one morning that April (driving the seventy-five miles there and back each day was taking its toll) I was approaching the office and slowed down at a junction where some new road works had been set up. I felt a bump at the back of my car. The driver behind me had not been expecting me to stop and had braked a little too late. As we both got out of our cars to exchange insurance details, I was somewhat flustered and not so much bothered about the small amount of damage to the boot (it was a company car!) as I was annoyed about the inconvenience and interruption to my plans for the day. I shouted at the poor man, "I haven't got time for this, I've just started a new job and I'm trying to get selected to stand in a by-election!"

The Labour Party has different rules for the selection of a candidate in a by-election. Because it is a high-profile event, attracting a lot of interest from the national media, the candidates of all parties receive much more attention than they do in a general election. The National Executive Committee therefore scrutinises the credentials of each applicant very carefully, even when it is unlikely that the party will win the seat. They quite rightly want to be sure that the party will be represented by a candidate who can speak up well for its policies and principles. They especially want to make sure that she or he has no skeletons in their cupboard. For these reasons the selection from the final shortlist is made not by the local party but by the NEC.

I was delighted and very excited to achieve a position on that final shortlist. There were only two other people on it, - one man and one woman. Did I have a chance? Was I making a mistake in even wanting to be the candidate in a by-election for a seat where there was no hope of winning? It could be a huge strategic error in my campaign to become an MP. Despite these doubts I still felt immensely proud to be called to attend the selection interview at Walworth Road in London, the then Party Headquarters. It was a very amicable affair, with the three of us hopefuls gathering before and afterwards for coffee and a chat. I was greeted in a very gentle way by the panel and found the questions from Margaret Beckett particularly encouraging. She seemed to find it amusing when I said, referring to my having stood and lost in Sevenoaks, that to lose in a general election where many others across the country were also losing was one thing, but to lose in a by-election under the full glare of national publicity would be quite another! She could see that at least I had no illusions about winning this seat if I were to be selected.

However, I did not get the chance to represent my party on this occasion. The selection was won by the man on the shortlist, a local Newbury man who was well known in the constituency and who deserved to win. The day after the selection interview I travelled to Llandudno in North Wales for the Party's annual Women's Conference. I gave a speech that day in which I told the assembled audience that I had failed to win the "poisoned chalice" of selection for the Newbury by-election. I got the impression that most of the delegates thought I had done myself a favour by failing to get selected and were wondering why I had even wanted it in the first place! My attempt to get selected for a by-election in an unwinnable seat had been a diversion and I needed to get back on track.

During the next few months of 1993 I bought a new home in Reading, cutting my last ties with Sevenoaks and went on to do my first in-depth personal development course in London, reaching my fiftieth birthday along the way. Ten years had passed since that critical year of 1983 and my world was still continuing to change as the Fridays came and went.

Chapter 14

The years spent chasing a winnable seat

"The best-laid schemes o' mice an' men gang aft agley."
Robert Burns

From 1994 until 1997 I was focussed on one thing: standing at the next general election in a winnable seat. Admittedly I hadn't been successful in achieving my aim of moving to the north of the country but that didn't stop me from seeking nominations from branches in constituencies far and wide, up and down and across the country. I had a car and I was willing to drive whatever the distance was. As soon as a possible winnable seat appeared in "Tribune" I was in gear, literally and metaphorically.

I was pleased to have a new photograph to insert into my CV. At the 1994 Conference I had had my picture taken with the newly elected leader of our party, Tony Blair. The opportunity had briefly presented itself while I was attending a UNISON reception. I had my camera with me and, seeing Tony Blair approaching, I thrust it into the hands of Hector Mackenzie, one of the three joint leaders of the newly formed UNISON, and asked him to take a photo of me shaking hands with Tony Blair. He obliged and I boldly walked up to Tony Blair and asked him to pose with me. In a moment I had seized the chance; it was sheer opportunism on my part. I had voted for Tony Blair to become leader earlier that summer, but it was for the same reason that many others had voted for him, - I thought he could win the next election for Labour. He himself had jokingly acknowledged this at a special conference I attended soon after his election as leader. Nevertheless I naively imagined that having a photograph on the front of my CV of me shaking hands with Tony Blair would help me in my quest to become a Member of Parliament.

Meeting Tony Blair at Labour Party Conference in Blackpool October 1994

Tweaking my CV to suit each respective constituency, I purchased numerous batches of brown A4 envelopes and stuffed them with dozens of copies to send to branches within the various constituencies. It was a scattergun approach, hardly the most efficient strategy. It resulted in a series of invitations to nominating meetings from branches all over the country, from as far north as North-West Leicestershire to as far south as Exeter in Devon. The purpose of attending these meetings was to collect a nomination from each branch within a constituency with a view to my inclusion on their final shortlist. Sometimes I would receive an invitation from only one branch within a constituency but I still went and gave my speech, no matter what the distance nor what time of day. The Exeter meeting took place at 8.00pm and after a full day's work I drove the hundred and forty miles from Reading along the A303, gave my speech and drove back, reaching home in the early hours of the morning.

By then I had learned a few lessons about what to wear for such meetings, not least because of the phenomenon known as "Folletting". Barbara Follett MP had become the Labour Party's dress guru, the Trini and Susannah of the day, and it was to her that many aspiring women MPs looked for advice on how to present themselves. While not actually attending one of her courses I did nevertheless pick up a few tips. It was amusing to note how many of us turned up at subsequent annual conferences sporting smart red suits and wearing black court shoes on our feet and little gold bangles on our wrists. "Spot the women hopefuls" was an easy game to play!

It was around this time that the Labour Party introduced the idea of all-women shortlists, a positive action strategy which was controversial both outside and inside the party. Contrary to popular opinion, the strategy would only operate in half, not all, of the winnable seats in the country, but it caused a furore. At that time women constituted less than ten per cent of Members of Parliament. The intention was to make it compulsory for certain constituencies to select a woman candidate for the next general election, thus giving a more balanced representation in parliament of the population as a whole. Being a lifelong feminist I naturally supported this policy. It also gave me the chance to speak at the party's annual conference in Blackpool in 1994, when the motion to introduce all-women shortlists was proposed. I would speak on the subject about which I felt most passionate. I wanted to make an impact and I did.

I simply told the story of my selection process for the 1992 General Election and how local parties frankly often failed to disguise their prejudice against women candidates. I told the conference that my clothes had sometimes been the deciding factor in my failing to get a seat and related the story about my costume being too severe. I told them how in the end I did get selected, - in the fourth safest Tory seat in the country! "We've got the vote," I said, "now we want the votes!" It brought the house down! I was amazed at the applause! As I stepped down from the platform I was dazzled by the sight and sound of camera flashbulbs popping as well as dozens of reporters, notebooks in hand, wanting interviews. I was in demand by the national press! The papers love anything to do with sex, and this was sexy. The following day my picture appeared in a double-page spread in the Daily Mirror, which was headlined "Give Women the Votes" and reported that I had given "one of the best performances from the conference floor all week"! The motion was carried and I was pleased to have played my part in this momentous chapter of women's participation in the Labour movement. But most of all I was on a high and I felt famous! Surely this would help me in my quest to become an MP?

A week later I entered a room in a building near the House of Commons to attend a meeting of "City 2020". This was an enquiry into urban regeneration and consisted of a panel of luminaries brought together the previous year by Keith Vaz MP to create a vision of cities for the future. It wasn't simply a talking shop; we made visits to various cities and held discussions with local dignitaries in places like Glasgow and Birmingham. Other members of the panel included Richard Rogers and Margaret Hodge (not yet an MP) and I had been invited to sit on this panel some months previously as a representative woman from the South! As I walked into the room Keith Vaz stood up and gave me a round of warm applause for my conference speech. He even gave himself some of the credit for my performance, saying it must have been my experience on the "City 2020" group that had enabled me to speak with such aplomb! Nevertheless I accepted his tribute gracefully.

Despite all this activity, after moving to my new home in Reading I was feeling somewhat isolated. I had moved to a new part of the country where I knew no-one apart from my new colleagues in UNISON. I was enjoying my job, which was challenging and demanding, involving a lot of travelling to branches situated as far apart as Milton Keynes, Banbury and Bournemouth and I would often return home late in the evenings. At weekends I was frequently running training courses in assertiveness and confidence-building. On a yearly basis I was organising the regional delegation to UNISON National Women's Conference as well as planning and delivering the annual Women's Conference of the Southern Region (later to be merged with the neighbouring region to become the South East Region). My work took up a great deal of my time and energy but I had not lost sight of my "grand plan". I soon started going to meetings of the local Labour Party and this helped me to become involved in the local community and get to know people other than my work colleagues.

There was one snag however about the location of the house I had bought. I had assumed, because my address was Reading, that I was living in the Constituency of Reading East where there was a thriving Branch Labour Party. However, I was living in a part of Reading called Earley and my house was situated two doors away from the border of Reading East; I was actually living in the Constituency of Wokingham, which was as staunch a Tory stronghold as Sevenoaks had ever been and where the MP was John Redwood! The local party was well used to putting up candidates only to watch them fail, just as the Sevenoaks party had done. I certainly felt at home there! However, despite now living within a similar type of constituency to the one I had just left I do not regret this move as I made some good and long-lasting friends in my local branch and in the constituency.

The following year I was persuaded to become a candidate in the local elections for Wokingham District Council. At that time there was only one Labour member on the council and she was standing down. I wasn't sure that this would necessarily help me in my long term objective to become an MP but I had a go and the Labour party lost the seat. I resisted all later attempts to persuade me to stand for Wokingham in the next Parliamentary election. I had already stood in a no-hoper and there was nothing to be gained by repeating the experience. I was looking for a winnable seat and

I would not be deterred from that goal, come what may. So I continued in my quest to get selected, travelling far and wide, giving speeches to Labour Party members all over the country telling them why I would be the best candidate for Swindon or Gloucester or wherever I had travelled to that day. I did not restrict myself to applying to those designated as all-women shortlists. When I telephoned each branch the following day for feedback on why I hadn't been successful in receiving their nomination I would often be told that I had given the best speech but the meeting had been packed with supporters of the local contender so I hadn't stood a chance. Usually that local person was a man.

  However in the end I did actually reach the final shortlist of three constituencies: Welwyn Hatfield, Slough and Gravesham, all with differing degrees of "winnability" and thus they stood a chance of going Labour at the next election. They were all-women shortlists. Now I felt I really did have a chance of surmounting the final hurdle and getting selected as a candidate with a realistic chance of becoming a Member of Parliament. Once more I travelled in great hope. The evening of the Welwyn Hatfield selection meeting proved to be a tense few hours until the decision was made but I hadn't got it. However, I consoled myself with the fact that this was the least winnable of the three and I prepared my speech for the next one, Slough. This was a very winnable seat but I knew that the likely candidate had worked the constituency very thoroughly over the past couple of years; it became clear to me and the rest of us on the shortlist that we were only there to make up the numbers. I was right. She won handsomely and deserved to do so. Gravesham was my last chance.

  It is a long drive from Reading in Berkshire to Gravesend in Kent and on the afternoon of Monday January 8th, 1996, I left work early and set off in my car with determination. I had the branch nominations, I had a good speech ready to deliver and I was going to give it my all. This was it; I would use my previous connections with Kent to good effect and I would do my best to become the next MP for Gravesham! Listening to my car radio as I drove along the M25 my attention was suddenly riveted by a newsflash.

An Industrial Tribunal had just ruled that Labour's policy of All-Women Shortlists was illegal; it contravened the Sex Discrimination Act of 1975, an Act of Parliament with which I was very familiar in my work. Any selection processes currently underway must be suspended. I was shocked. What to do now? Should I just leave the motorway at the next junction and turn around and drive home again? What was the point in carrying on? I had of course been aware that two men who had been prevented from standing on certain shortlists were challenging Labour Party policy in court but there had been many threats of legal action and even though this case had got as far as an Industrial Tribunal I had not seriously thought they would win. It was hard to take it in. I decided to drive on to the selection meeting and see what awaited me there.

On my arrival in Gravesham the constituency secretary greeted me with "Have you heard the news?" It was all over. The constituency officers went through the motions that evening, with the other two women hopefuls looking just as rueful as I must have looked. Our hearts were no longer in it. With no voting taking place that evening the meeting was soon over and I was back on the M25 heading towards Reading with my bubble burst.

The maximum amount of time allowed between general elections in this country is five years. It was now nearly four years since the 1992 election and time was running out. Most of the Parliamentary selections had already taken place and the prospective candidates were already working their constituencies. The next election could be called at any time. I made a few last half-hearted attempts at a couple of the remaining constituencies that were still to select a candidate but as the remaining months went by I began to accept that there was little chance for me now. The all-women shortlists had been my best hope. It was widely and correctly assumed that Labour would win the next election and it would have provided me with the best chance I would ever have of becoming an MP. The Tories had been in power for four terms and New Labour with its bright new leader was poised to seize the reins.

The PPC (Prospective Parliamentary Candidate) for Wokingham was already in place. She had been selected some months previously and had my full support. I knew what she was facing as she strove valiantly to fly the Labour flag in an unwinnable constituency. When at last the General Election was duly called in April 1997, to take place on May 1st, I was still trying to reconcile myself to the fact that whether the Labour Party won or lost, I was not going to become a Member of Parliament.

The Wokingham candidate stayed at my house for the latter part of the four-week campaign and on the night of May 1st she and I attended the Count at the local leisure centre. As we waited for our local result to be announced, which we knew was a forgone conclusion for John Redwood, we kept our eyes on the television screens outside the hall. Our joy at the developing Labour landslide was a wonderful antidote to the familiar feeling of resignation as we witnessed the victory of the local Tory MP for Wokingham. After the formalities of the candidates' speeches we drove home as the dawn was breaking and the milk was arriving on my doorstep.

On Friday May 2nd, after a short sleep, I watched the miracle continuing to unfold on television. After eighteen long years this country had a Labour Government once again. My delight however was tempered by my own personal disappointment in failing to obtain a seat. There they all were, a hundred and one Labour women MPs, some of whom I knew personally, all taking their places on those green benches and I wasn't among them. Welwyn Hatfield, Slough and Gravesham all came over to Labour, (Gravesham, incidentally, being won by a man).

Although I had of course known for some months that I wasn't going to be there the stark reality of the situation still hit me with some force. This was so different from how I had felt on that Friday morning after the 1992 election. On that day I had been expecting to be rejoicing at a Labour victory while accepting my own personal defeat and so had been doubly affected by the party's failure to win. On the Friday morning after the 1997 election however, I felt a huge conflict within me. Of course I was happy to see Labour in power once more; of course I rejoiced with party members and UNISON colleagues. But inside I was weeping for a lost cause, a failed mission. Labour was at the zenith of its power and I had missed the boat. The next election four or five years from then would surely see the party lose seats and if there had ever been a chance for me this would have been it. I had failed.

PART THREE
1993-2012

CHANGING MYSELF

"I wanted to change the world. But I have found that the only thing one can be sure of changing is oneself."

Aldous Huxley.

Chapter 15

What did I really want?

"When you change the way you look at things, the things you look at change."
Wayne Dyer

I don't regret trying to stand for a winnable seat. All that striving and yearning, all that travelling and speech-making, all those red suits and little black court shoes. There was never any guarantee that I would have won but I'd had a dream and I had gone after it. It was a rich experience. If this were simply a story about how I failed to become a Member of Parliament it would end here with a list of lessons for future parliamentary hopefuls to take away:

>1. Make a strategic plan.
>2. Target a small number of constituencies (just one if you are very brave).
>3. Get to know the local area by spending time there.
>4. Make contact with the local opinion-makers.
>5. Build up a network of support from inside the local party.
>6. Most of all know what you want and be sure it really is what you want.

I had done none of these things.

My personal journey was still in progress however. Without being fully aware of it, I had already been taking a few steps along a very different path. Soon after leaving teaching to start my new career as a union official and a new life at my home in

Reading I spent a week in London on a personal development course called "Insight". It was the summer of 1993 and I was almost fifty years old. Before I left teaching I had already trained to become a qualified assertiveness-trainer; this came about as part of my work on equal opportunities with Kent County Council. The authority had agreed to fund a "Training the Trainers" course for ten teachers throughout the county and I had been one of them. I subsequently ran a number of courses for teachers and the basic principles of assertiveness were now second nature to me. A self-development course seemed to be the next obvious direction in which to go as it promised to deliver a deeper insight into myself. I knew nothing about what I was letting myself in for and I just plunged in. I booked a week of my annual leave and told my colleagues I was going on holiday as I was too embarrassed to tell anyone what I was really going to do. Notions of self-development did not fit well with hard-nosed trade unionism.

The course took place in a hotel in London and my room number was 101 which seemed very significant to me. There were a number of similar courses being held around the country at that time, all with different degrees of rigour and severity. Mine was probably one of the lighter ones; nevertheless it was like nothing I had ever experienced. The sessions took place in a large room, with around a hundred participants agreeing on a contract. No smoking, coffee or alcohol was permitted throughout the week (even in out-of-course hours) and strict rules of punctuality and confidentiality were enforced. It was a life-changing week. There were tears and laughter, fun and sadness. Many personal stories were exchanged and we all learned from one another as well as discovering aspects of our own inner selves which surprised, frightened and delighted us in equal measure. I could hardly believe that I was doing this. How liberating it was! If my sister could see me now, I thought, she wouldn't believe that I could behave so "out of character"!

It was while chatting with some of the other participants that I learned about a special kind of holiday centre in Greece called "Skyros" which ran "alternative" holidays on the Greek

Island of the same name, situated in the Sporades. The brochure described courses in personal development, music, writing, yoga and tai chi and after not a great deal of deliberation I plucked up the courage to book a fortnight's holiday there the following summer. This was a big step for me. I had never been abroad on my own and I was both excited and nervous.

    I had flown in aeroplanes on only four occasions in my life. The first was in 1977 when at the age of thirty-three I went to the USA with my husband and children to visit his sister in Rochester, New York State. This was my first time in an aeroplane and I was in a jumbo jet on a transatlantic flight! What made it all the more surprising to me and to my family was the fact that I had always been somewhat claustrophobic, even to the extent of avoiding stepping into a lift! The next time I ventured inside an aeroplane was in 1983 when at the age of thirty-nine I was on a flight to Jersey for my first NUT Conference, accompanied and supported by colleagues. I knocked back a few vodkas at the airport to get my courage up for that one. On the third occasion, in December 1990 at the age of forty-eight, I flew to Dortmund to spend the New Year holiday with my soldier boyfriend; I did actually manage the journey on my own but he met me at the other end. The most recent occasion had been my flight to Argentina two years previously but I had been accompanied by my then partner, my parliamentary agent. So to fly on my own to Greece, a country I had never visited, to share a fortnight with people I had never met and to take part in some "alternative" holiday was a big deal for me. After checking in at Heathrow I waited patiently for some time for my flight to be called, forgetting that I hadn't yet been through security or passport control. Once I realised this I had to run fast to reach the departure gate in time to board my flight!

    The journey to Skyros was long and complicated. It involved a flight to Athens with an overnight stay in a hotel room shared with another course participant who was unknown to me and who had been allocated at random. (I discovered later that she was a member of the House of Lords!) The transfer from Athens to Skyros Island involved a coach journey to the coast, a ferry to the island of Evia, another coach across Evia to the shore at Kymi and a large ferry from Kymi to Linaria on Skyros Island. The final twenty minutes of this five-hour transfer was on foot to the Skyros Centre. I felt that I had travelled to the end of the earth. This was an adventure in itself. And I hadn't even started on the inner journey that was to come.

I signed up for a course called "Choose Life at Any Risk", led by Ari Badaines, a gestalt psychotherapist whose name I had never heard of and about whose methods I knew nothing. In short I had no idea what to expect. Psychodrama was a new word to me. As I entered the course room on the first morning, I was prepared (but not ready) for whatever might occur. It was a light, airy room and we were a small group. Eight of us tentatively walked in and made our way to the very comfortable, cushioned seats arranged in a semicircle facing our course leader. We waited in silence for the introductory exercise to begin. We waited and we waited and we waited but Ari said nothing at all. We just sat looking at him, at each other and at the floor in a very awkward and embarrassed silence, shifting every now and again on our cushions. It seemed to me as if this silence would never end but eventually, to my relief, someone at last found the courage to say something; the silence was broken and the group process gradually began to flow.

The most significant thing for me about the processes involved during that week occurred not during the course hours but later one night. For some reason (which I can't remember but which must have been very persuasive) Ari Badaines suggested that I set my alarm for 3.00am, get out of bed, sit on a chair on the balcony of my room and quietly meditate. This I duly did. Making sure that I had drunk no alcohol that evening I responded promptly to my alarm clock and sat on a hard chair for twenty minutes in the cool night air of that Greek Island, pondering life, the Universe and everything.

The next morning I reported in to the course session, proudly telling everyone that I had carried out the mission assigned to me. The response I received from Ari was not the one of admiration which I had expected. There was no applause, no gold star for being a good pupil. Instead he asked me why I had done it. I was baffled; it was obvious to me why I had done it; he had set me the task and I was doing it because he had told me to. "You didn't HAVE to do it", he boomed, "You had a choice; you could have chosen NOT to do it!" His words were like a bombshell. I had never even considered that! What an eye-opener that was! Yes, I now realised, I really did have a choice. And yet, being the obedient person that I was, I had spent the previous evening in a state of anxiety about having to get up in the middle of the night and I had disturbed my sleep in order to comply with something I had perceived as an order. This was surely a command for which I would earn Brownie points if I carried it out successfully, I had thought. I now understood that I could have chosen to ignore or flout Ari's suggestion, which I had interpreted as an order, but this was an option which had not occurred to me. I had learned a profound lesson, one which was to stay with me always. Everything we do in our lives is a result of the choices we make and it is always an error to imagine that we have no other options in the decisions we make and the actions we take. On the contrary we always have a myriad of possible choices within our power and once we recognise this we open the door to freedom.

A few years later when I was talking to a colleague about these ideas, asserting that we always have a choice in everything we do, she became very defensive. "I don't have a choice about whether I come to work or not," she said. "I have a mortgage to pay and therefore of course I have to work." I said that she could have chosen not to take on a mortgage, or maybe found some other way of obtaining the money to pay for it, like gambling or marrying a very rich man! The examples may have been far-fetched but my point was that we do not "have to" do anything, that all our actions and decisions are based on choices which reflect our values and priorities. My colleague was not convinced; to her it was a given, a *sine qua non*: she "had to" come to work and she had no choice in the matter. It wasn't until I trained as a Louise Hay teacher a few years later that these ideas were further reinforced and I came to understand that as well as our actions and decisions we also choose our thoughts and our beliefs. These choices may not always be conscious ones but they are choices nevertheless.

As I progressed along my journey of personal change during the following years I continued to make further interesting discoveries while reflecting on my earlier life choices. I was gradually beginning to realise that maybe at my inner core I hadn't really wanted to become a Member of Parliament after all, or at least not wanted it enough. I had convinced myself at some level that if I secured myself a seat on those green benches I could, even as a backbencher, contribute to making changes in certain areas of legislation which were important to me, like discrimination, equality and prejudice. I knew for certain that I wanted to make changes in the world, to make a difference in some way and I had already had some practice in making changes to small parts of the world around me. I had helped to give people in Sevenoaks more access to their local swimming pool through a local referendum and I had persuaded Kent County Council to declare itself an Equal Opportunities Employer and to introduce job-share and career-break schemes. I had felt proud of these achievements and knew from first-hand experience that it was possible for a group of committed people to bring about improvements in the lives of others. It was this knowledge which spurred me on in chasing a winnable seat for all those years, and the inevitable ego-boost which accompanied the pursuit was undeniably an added factor.

However, I was now beginning to have doubts about whether I had truly desired the prize (that of becoming an MP) which I was seeking. Maybe there was something unconsciously holding me back. Maybe I hadn't wanted it badly enough. Maybe I hadn't really believed I could achieve it. Even though I had done all those affirmations, even though I had created the treasure maps advocated in all those self-help books I had read and on all those the courses I had attended, I still had not reached the pot of gold at the end of the rainbow. Perhaps it wasn't what I really, really wanted after all.

I first learned about the power of affirmations when I read "Feel the Fear and Do It Anyway" by Susan Jeffers and I had put these into practice when pursuing my goal to be an MP. As I drove to each of the nominating meetings I would shout out at the top of my voice in the privacy of my car, "I am powerful and I am loved!" over and over again. Then later I would chant, "I am the next MP for Slough" (or Swindon or whichever constituency I was driving to)! It certainly helped me to feel confident but I learned that confidence is not the only requirement in the quest to become a Member of Parliament. My treasure maps didn't work the magic either. I had collected a large number of postcards showing photographs of the House of Commons, both interior and exterior shots, past and present and had made a collage of them, which I put in a frame and hung on my bedroom wall. In the centre I had stuck the photograph of me shaking hands with Tony Blair, and I had superimposed a smaller picture of me on the green benches, so it looked as though I had already achieved my goal. Wow, I thought, that would surely work!

What I came to understand when I studied to become an NLP Practitioner in 2003 was that unless you have honestly answered that most basic question "What do you want?" and honed it right down until you discover the values and beliefs which run your life, no amount of tinkering with affirmations, treasure maps and so forth will help. If you are going in a direction which does not sit comfortably with your own inner strengths and values you will be chasing an unrealisable dream. It was a slow and painful lesson I was learning but when I finally accepted it I also experienced a degree of relief. I did not have to keep trying to impress people, I did not always have to say the right things and toe the party line; I did not have to show a strong and determined face to the world. I could choose not to do any of those things and I could now be a more authentic version of myself.

Chapter 16

My father speaks to me

"All I can do is be me, whoever that is."
Bob Dylan

It took me two years after the Labour Party's triumph on that morning of Friday 1st May, 1997, to fully accept the reality of the collapse of my dream to become an MP. Perhaps it was no coincidence that it was around that time that I made some discoveries about my family history which helped me to explore my own identity and eventually to find a more authentic direction to my life.

One evening in March 1997, just prior to the General Election, I was making dinner for myself at home after a day's work. I had been visiting one of the many UNISON branches for which I was responsible as Regional Women's Officer when the telephone rang. I picked up the receiver, expecting to have one of my regular and very welcome chats with my son or my daughter. I heard a man's voice saying, "Are you Jeannie Benjamin, the daughter of Eric Arthur Benjamin?"

I gasped and sat down abruptly. The mention of my father's name coupled with the use of my maiden name sent a shiver through my body. I was still using my married name of Evans at that time and hadn't been called Jeannie Benjamin for the last thirty-one years. My whole body shook as I sat down on my settee; I felt that I was being addressed by my father's ghost. After a pause I said yes I was. The man told me that his name was Mr Couldrey and he explained that he was a genealogist working on behalf of a cousin of my father who was in a psychiatric nursing home and who was unable to make a will on his own behalf. Mr Couldrey went on to say that he needed to track down all the members of the family so that the Official Solicitor at the Court of Protection could draw up a will. He informed me that I had close relations in England and in Canada, all of whom were related to me on my father's side, and of whom I knew nothing. There was one woman in particular, called Frances, who was another of my father's cousins, who had been doing some genealogical research in an effort to try and find all the members of the family prior to this. I gave him the other details he wanted, the name of my sister and her address (he did not know I had a sister) and then he told me that my Great, Great Grandfather was called Moses. My mother had often mentioned to Sally and me that we must have some Jewish heritage because of the name Benjamin. I had always felt a strong Jewish connection and so to learn that I had an ancestor called Moses just clinched it!

I could hardly take this all in. My father's cousin, the genealogist told me, was called François Benjamin, again someone I had never heard of and he was in a nursing home in Sandhurst, just a few miles from where I was living in Reading! I busily scribbled down all this information on a scrap of paper although Mr Couldrey had told me he would follow up his call with a letter. I thanked him rather weakly, put the phone down and burst into tears! It was truly as though my father had contacted me through the ether and across the years. After taking some moments to reflect and to try and assimilate this incredible news I rang first my sister and then the man with whom I was in a relationship at the time; he was a gardener at Reading University and a UNISON member and I had met him while running an assertive training course for UNISON members. I needed to talk and he listened.

Soon after this I received a letter from Frances, the relation in Canada whom he had mentioned. (I had given him permission to give her my address.) In the letter she told me that she and her husband Mark were in England carrying out research into the family tree and they were keen to get in touch with me. They wanted to contact me by phone before they left the country and asked whether I would be willing to pass on my number to them through Mr Couldrey, which I did. Unfortunately however, it turned out that they did not get my message in time and were already on their way back to Canada (passing through Reading station as they later told me)!

During that phone call from Mr Couldrey I was told about my other, very close, relatives of whom I knew nothing at all. Apparently I had two first cousins, sisters, who were of a similar age to me and my sister and who were living not far away in Surrey. They also had known nothing of my or my sister's existence. They were the daughters of my father's only sister, Queenie, whose real name was Victoria. I have wondered since then whether my father christened me Jeannie as an echo of his sister's name. My mother had always told me that I was named after my father's favourite song of the time, "I dream of Jeannie with the light brown hair", but maybe there was another more subconscious reason for my name; I will never know. I do remember hearing the name Queenie occasionally as I was growing up but only in whispers. Queenie was known as the "black sheep" of my father's family. She had left home to go off with a married man and had become pregnant. As a result she was ostracised and never spoken of within the family circle again. My father also had two brothers, Ernest and Leslie, whom we did know about and who used to visit us once a year at Christmas with their wives and sons, but sadly we never met Queenie and we never knew about any children.

I made contact with my new-found cousins by telephone and they were delighted; they told me they were extremely pleased to discover that they had some wider family members because they had always felt totally alone while they were growing up. Over the next few months we learned more about our respective families. There were many similarities; their names were not unlike ours, Sylvia and Joan as opposed to Jeannie and Sally; they were born in 1942 and 1944, we were born in 1943 and 1945, and they, like us, had been educated at a Catholic convent school. What emerged was that their mother Queenie (who, like their father had died in 1970), had married their father after his first wife had died and because of the earlier shame of their mother's pregnancy Sylvia and Joan were brought up without any knowledge of their extended family. However, as they grew up their mother often used to tell them that she had a favourite brother called Eric and that he held a special place in her heart. But they were as unaware of us, Eric's children, as Sally and I were of them. The difference was that whereas they had always felt quite alone in the world and had known nothing of any wider family, Sally and I had grown up surrounded by a large family of aunts, uncles and cousins on our mother's side.

**Our first meeting with our "new" cousins
(L to R: Sally, Joan, Charlotte, Sylvia, me)
August 31st 1997**

That summer my sister Sally, my daughter Charlotte and I arranged to meet our new cousins, Sylvia and Joan. They had invited us to lunch at Sylvia's home in Coulsdon, near Croydon on the Bank Holiday weekend of Sunday August 31st, 1997. The previous night there had been a car crash in Paris and as we awoke we learned with the rest of the world of the death of Diana, Princess of Wales. Somehow it seemed an auspicious day to be connecting with our new-found family. Although not a royalist I was nevertheless caught up in the shock of the news, particularly when Charlotte arrived from her home in London telling us about the huge spread of flowers she had seen outside Kensington Palace. I discovered that my cousins were keen royalists and I am sure that if we had not been visiting them that day Sylvia and Joan would have been watching all the news coverage as it unfolded. However, they were perfect hosts and put on a wonderful lunch for us. Sylvia's husband, daughter, son-in-law and two little granddaughters (one of whom was also called Charlotte) joined us later and we spent the afternoon piecing together our respective family histories and marvelling at our strong family resemblance. Over the following years we began to know our cousins better and we now keep in touch regularly, even though they have since moved permanently to Spain.

When I met François Benjamin later that year it was an altogether different experience. I had been told by the genealogist that François had been diagnosed as a "bizarre psychotic" and that I couldn't expect to get much sense out of him. In fact he was a schizophrenic. He was sixty-nine years old and had lived all his adult life in nursing homes or psychiatric hospitals. I had previously contacted Harts Leap nursing home where he now lived, to let them know that I was a bona fide relative of the man they were caring for and that he was my father's first cousin, which meant I was his first cousin once removed. I set out by myself one Sunday afternoon to drive the short distance to Sandhurst to meet the man who was from the same generation as the father I had only known for the first eighteen months of my life. I took with me a present of St Bruno tobacco. I had discovered that this was François' favourite pipe tobacco after Mr Couldrey had put me in touch with a Mr Philip Warner who had apparently maintained a long interest in the welfare of François, having known him in his early years.

The nursing home was a dreary place. I had never been anywhere like it. I introduced myself to the member of staff on duty and he took me down dark, narrow corridors which smelled of disinfectant, into a communal sitting room. All the residents were arranged on chairs around the edge of the room, either staring into nothingness or at the television or calling out some unintelligible words in an attempt to attract the attention of the staff. I was led across the room to a man sitting by the window. He had quite a distinguished look about him, with a deep frown and a long grey beard (which was shaven off by my next visit). The member of staff told him who I was and left me with him. François was not at all impressed with me, although he did grant me a brief smile. He soon began what was to become one of his familiar monologues: a huge outpouring of tales of horror and savagery. Unintelligible stories about blood, violence and gore tumbled out of his mouth, how he aimed his rifle and started shooting everyone, bang, bang, bang, the walls were splattered, everyone was dead, there was lots and lots of blood; all of this was delivered at a great rate of words per minute. My efforts at polite conversation were not a match for the speed and graphic imagery of his tales of destruction and violence. I gave him the present of St Bruno pipe tobacco and after twenty minutes I took my leave, saying I would be back with some of his other relatives next time. He showed no interest in the prospect of future visitors.

I drove home feeling somewhat shattered and disappointed. If I had been hoping to hear any memories he may have had of my father as a child, those hopes were certainly dashed from the first moment of our meeting. However, I had done it; I had satisfied my curiosity. I had felt it my duty to visit this man, who had never had anyone come to see him, and who after all was a blood relative. Moreover I did actually feel very sorry for him. I knew that I would be going to see him regularly from then on and that I would bring my sister and my two "new" cousins to see him in the future.

On the next occasion however, I was again on my own. It followed a similar pattern, with more tales of guns, bloodthirsty violence and rage interspersed with the odd, incongruous but charming smile. At the end of this visit however, as I got into the driving seat of my car I felt a warm dampness seeping through my trousers. I had been sitting next to François on a chair which must have been recently occupied by an incontinent resident and because the chair was warm I had not noticed the dampness until I sat down again in my car. I hastily put a newspaper between me and the seat of my car and drove home at double speed until I could take off my clothes and get under the shower!

**Our first meeting with François, my father's cousin
(L to R: Me, Joan, Sally, Sylvia)
Spring 1998**

François' story is a tragic one. He was brought up in Eastbourne, Sussex, by his French mother, Anne-Marie Thérèse and his English father, Ernest Victor, my father's uncle. His mother was a staunch Catholic and François was sent to Downside Abbey, an independent Catholic boarding school for boys near Bath, run by Benedictine monks. While he was there a tragic incident occurred. In May 1943, when François was fourteen years old, an aeroplane crashed on to the school playing fields while the boys were playing cricket. Nine of the boys were killed. François had witnessed this terrible accident at first hand and it was this which had subsequently caused his mental illness. In those times it was standard procedure to treat such an illness with surgery and consequently a lobotomy was performed on François' brain. As a result of this he spent most of the rest of his life in institutions.

The account of the plane crash is recorded by Dom Hubert Van Zeller, then Chaplain of Downside, in "Downside By and Large", published by Sheed and Ward in 1953. On page 159 he writes:

"The summer term of this year (1943) was darkened by the most notable disaster that the School has yet suffered: the accidental death of nine boys and the injury of many others. On the afternoon of May 15th, when everyone was on the cricket field for the opening First Eleven match, an aeroplane crashed on the top bank and burst into flames. The engine smashed the side wall of the pavilion, much heavy metal breaking off and striking the boys who were taken completely off their guard. The pilot was killed outright. The effect on the whole place – boys, masters, monks – cannot be described. The sense of speechless mourning, even more poignant than the outward ceremonies which followed, will not be forgotten by those who lived through those sad days of common loss."

There is a later, much more detailed account provided in a letter to Frances, my father's Canadian cousin, in 1997, when she was doing some research into family history. The letter comes from Dom Philip Jebb, then archivist at Downside Abbey, who had witnessed the crash while a pupil at the school and escaped death by a few feet. He tells of François being withdrawn from the school a year early in March 1946 suffering from an acute and serious anxiety state, and of François talking about being shot at and having a craze for daggers. Included with Dom Philip Jebb's letter is a long description of the events of May 15th 1943, which he had written in 1993 for the fiftieth anniversary of the event.

From this account it appears that there were two aeroplanes which were engaged in a training programme. They were Hurricane fighters from Yeovilton Fleet Air Arm base and it was the second plane which made a very low pass and crashed into the boys. Detailing the deaths and injuries of all the boys, Father Jebb recounts:

"This makes a total of thirty-three boys physically and seriously affected by the crash. Many others were slightly hurt, and this takes no account of the emotional and psychological harm arising from shock."

He also mentions a boy called Philip Warner, who provided a written account of the accident for the Headmaster the next day. Philip Warner was the man whose name I had been given by the genealogist and who had taken such a long-standing interest in the welfare of François. This was the man I had spoken to on the phone and who had told me about François' liking for St Bruno tobacco. I hadn't realised until I read Father Jebb's account what a close connection Philip Warner had had with François when they were boys and I now felt that I had a real tangible connection to my father's cousin. On the day of the accident Philip Warner had been reading a book on the east side of the Pavilion, (*"not being interested in cricket"*) and he immediately went to help. This is part of his story:

"I met Kirkpatrick limping, and Harvey helping him along...I saw Klein lying on a bench, with his face full of blood, joking and gaily discussing with a man I did not know, whether he had a fracture or not. On the next bench was a boy I could not recognise, whose face was terribly burnt; Mr Moore was tending him. There were no deck chairs. I looked round the corner; the flames had not abated; there was a body without a head lying on the ground. An Army man asked me to help push a car out of the way of the fire and smoke. This we did."

Perhaps it is not so surprising that François retained these horrific images in his mind for all those years and replayed them over and over again to anyone within earshot.

François died on Monday December 22nd, 2003, aged seventy-five. A week earlier I had been notified that he had suddenly become ill and had been taken to Frimley Park Hospital in Surrey so I took the afternoon off work and went to visit him there. He showed no interest in me. During the six years since we first learned of François' existence Sylvia, Joan, Sally and I had visited him regularly in the nursing home, particularly on his birthday and at Christmas, and the final time we saw him was in the hospital two days before he died. He showed no pleasure at the sight of us; on the contrary he shouted at us vehemently from his bed, telling us in no uncertain terms to go away! The only mourners at his funeral on Thursday January 15th, 2004, were the four of us cousins and my daughter Charlotte. It was a sad and pathetic occasion.

There is a poignant postscript to François' death. I had taken on the responsibility of arranging his funeral and since I had no instructions to the contrary I organised a cremation which took place in Slough. This was the most convenient place for the nursing home where he had lived and the hospital where he had died. Soon after he had been cremated however, it came to light that François' mother had expressed a wish in her will to the effect that not only should his funeral take the form of a burial but that he should be buried in the same grave as her and her husband, which was in Eastbourne. And I had already had him cremated!

I now felt somewhat guilty and wanted to make amends for my unintentional error and to reunite François with his parents in death. Their grave was situated in Ocklynge Cemetery, Eastbourne, which was the area in which they had lived. I collected the casket containing his ashes from the funeral directors in Slough and kept it in my house until I could make the necessary arrangements for the burial of the ashes. I learned that the protocol in Catholic circles is to have a Mass said for the deceased prior to any burial of ashes so I contacted my local church for this to be done and Sally and I attended this Mass. I made enquiries of the local authority in Eastbourne and eventually, on Monday May 10th, 2004, after much correspondence with the local authority and many formalities, François' ashes were duly buried in his parents' grave. A local priest conducted a short ceremony in the presence of me, my sister and an official from Eastbourne Borough Council. During this ceremony I noticed that on top of the grave there was an extra blank stone tablet which looked as though it had been designed to take an inscription for François. I am pleased to say that the tablet is no longer blank; below the names of François' parents it now reads "And their son François Ernest Benjamin, 29 May 1928 – 22 December 2003". I was glad to have played my part in reuniting them.

There was of course also the practical matter of the distribution of François' estate according to his will. As a representative of the family I had attended a meeting at the Court of Protection in November 1998 for the reading of the will, so the sum each of us was due to receive came as no surprise. François' fortune was considerable but so was his extended family; each person received an amount according to their generational position on the family tree. For the four of us cousins, who were a generation below François, this came to a few thousand pounds each. It wasn't a life-changing sum but we were grateful.

My other "new" relatives living in Canada, with whom I had been in regular email contact during all these formalities, were keen to maintain the contact we had established, especially Frances, François' first cousin. Frances had felt a close affinity with him, not simply because she was a first cousin but especially because of the similarity of their names. She and I had spoken on the phone for the first time soon after I had found out about her existence. She sounded a very gentle and warm woman and had a delightful soft Canadian accent. She also had a very keen interest in genealogy and had been researching our whole family history for many years. On her visit to England in 1997, before I had known about her, she had visited many relatives still living in this country, including François. We kept in contact regularly after that by phone and email and she sent me many parcels containing family photographs, letters and other information which she had been collecting for many years. She even sent me photographs of my father and letters written by him. It was all such a revelation to me. A phone call out of the blue from a genealogist in 1997 had led to a trail of discovery which I could never have foreseen and to revelations which continue to astonish me. A couple of years after François' death I would make a special trip to Vancouver Island to meet Frances and many other relatives who had settled there. But before then further discoveries would be made and more changes were still to happen.

Chapter 17

Learning to love myself

"When you change your thoughts, you change your life."
Louise L. Hay.

Becoming a Louise Hay Teacher in the summer of 1999 was one of the most significant steps in my journey of personal change. I was idly looking through the Guardian newspaper one lunch time while eating a sandwich at my office desk when a small boxed advertisement jumped out at me. It said very little other than "Come and train to be a Louise Hay teacher," giving the location (Birmingham) and the length of the course, (one week in July). I rang immediately to ask for more details which were subsequently sent through the post. I still find it astonishing that this tiny advertisement should have caught my attention so dramatically. I had only read one book by Louise Hay, "You Can Heal Your Life", and I had not even read it recently. It had not registered in my mind as anything more significant than the many other self-help books which I had been reading over the past few years (notably "The Celestine Prophecy" by James Redfield) and it certainly had not made such an impression as Susan Jeffers' "Feel the Fear and Do It Anyway". However I was very excited by the sudden appearance of this opportunity in my life and I had no hesitation in signing up for this one-week residential course.

It was a life-changing week, not least because I had a brief liaison with another course participant, an ex-priest. I recalled afterwards to a work colleague that the affair (if it could be called that) had been a microcosm in which I had met, been attracted to, become close to, and finally fallen out of love with, a man whom I hardly knew, all within the space of a week! Of course the processes of self-discovery inherent in the course had had much to do with the rapid development and final ending of this short relationship. I was very grateful for the advice and help of the course leader, Dr. Patricia Crane, who had herself studied under Louise Hay. Dr. Crane provided some valuable counselling just when I needed it.

The aim of the course was to give participants an experience of a two-day workshop called "Love Yourself, Heal Your Life", and then to train us in how to deliver this workshop to others. This appealed to me greatly since I was well used to delivering assertiveness-training courses to UNISON members and previously to teachers. I was confident of my skills in the area of assertiveness and confidence-building and hoped I would be able to transfer them to this new arena.

The main tenets of the Louise Hay philosophy can be summed up in two basic presuppositions. The first is that if we want our lives to be fulfilled and happy then first and foremost we must love ourselves. The second is that an individual's thoughts and beliefs are the result of personal choice: although our parents and our culture will have had their influences we can nevertheless choose what to accept and what to reject. These are two very simple yet profound precepts.

Affirmations hold a central position within the theoretical framework of this belief system. Essentially they are anything we may say or think; more precisely they are statements which we make (either verbally or as unspoken thoughts) which may not be true at the moment we say them or think them but which we would like to be true. As I have often told students on my courses over the years since then, there are three important principles to remember about affirmations: they must be positive, they must be stated in the present tense and they must be personal.

First it is important to frame what we want in positive terms as the mind can only interpret a negative concept in a positive way. The traditional example used to illustrate this principle goes something like this: tell someone *not* to think of a yellow elephant with pink stripes and then ask them what image has come into their mind; of course it is that very same elephant! The brain cannot process the word "not". Secondly, as long as we say that something we want *will* become true it will always remain out there in the future and we will always be running after it trying to catch it up, therefore it must be phrased in the present tense as though it were already true.

The third principle to remember is to express the affirmation in a personal way by using the pronoun "I". We cannot do an affirmation on behalf of someone else and expect them to change; it is only ourselves we can change. As I absorbed these principles I began to see the wisdom of those famous words attributed to Mahatma Gandhi, "Be the change you wish to see in the world".

Some of the tenets of this philosophy can be hard to accept and certainly I struggled with them at the beginning. I found it particularly hard to put into practice the concept of forgiveness: that it is absolutely imperative to forgive those who have wronged you and even more so to forgive yourself. This can be a lifetime's work. The processes and exercises I underwent during that week of training were often extremely challenging, both intellectually and emotionally. However, I completed the course and was pleased to receive my certificate at the end of it.

I came home with an enthusiasm and a determination to put this new qualification to good use and while still working full-time for Unison I began to advertise and run weekend courses called "Love Yourself, Heal Your Life". It was then that another of the many "co-incidences" that were appearing in my life occurred; or were they rather instances of synchronicity? Firstly the South East Regional Office of the Labour Party had recently relocated to new premises on the left hand side of the UNISON Regional Office where I was working and secondly the director of the Therapy Centre in Reading, with whom I had already made contact, decided that she wanted to move it from central Reading to a quieter location. The property she chose was on the right hand side of the UNISON office. To me this seemed very propitious and symbolic.

I was working in a building which was situated in between a symbol of my past life on the left (the Labour Party) and a symbol of my possible future life on the right (Personal Development Training). Until then I had been trying out various locations for my courses in places like village halls and schools. Now I had a ready-made location in which to run my courses: next door to my present workplace. This was extremely convenient as I was able to use the shared car park; the Therapy Centre itself was also an ideal environment, having a large course room with a lovely peaceful atmosphere and a kitchen for refreshments. My weekend courses flourished there. I used the local "alternative" media, which were very much part of the Reading scene at that time, to attract people and I was building up a good practice. (I had also registered myself with the income tax people as self-employed in addition to my main employment which of course meant filling in a self-assessment tax return each year!)

At the beginning of this year I had also reclaimed my original name and on New Year's Eve 1999 I gave a party to celebrate my "rebirth". I had retained my married name of Evans for twelve years since getting divorced and I was now ready to be reunited with the name of Benjamin. During that time I had told myself that I was holding on to my married name both to provide continuity for my children (even though they were approaching adulthood at the time of the divorce) and also to avoid any confusion on my political CV as I pursued my quest for a seat in parliament. Neither of those reasons was now compelling (if they ever were). What was I holding on to? It was now time for the name of Benjamin to resume its rightful place in my life.

The discoveries I had recently made about my father's side of the family were a huge part of the rationale for my making this change. Even though as a feminist I recognised that women never truly possess their own names, only ever having the name of their husband or their father, this was the nearest I could get to it and it felt wonderful! I was no longer Mrs Evans; I was once again Ms Benjamin. Many of my friends asked me if it was expensive to change my name through Deed Poll and I explained that no legal procedure had been necessary as I was simply taking back something that was mine anyway. All I had to do was to let everyone know that henceforth I was to be known as Jeannie Benjamin. My colleagues adapted to the change quickly and my boss had the nameplate on my office door replaced to announce my new identity. There was one amusing moment when I took a phone call from a UNISON member who had heard about my name change: she was calling to congratulate me on my marriage!

Chapter 18

It's amazing what a visit to Thailand can do for life.

"There are no mistakes, no coincidences. All events are blessings given to us to learn from."
Elisabeth Kübler-Ross

In January 2001 I was ready to undertake further personal development work on myself and I embarked on another Skyros holiday. This time I was accompanied by my dear friend Marigold. She and I had met on my first Skyros holiday in 1994 and had been friends ever since. We had discovered we both lived in Reading so we saw each other regularly during the following years. The holiday we took together in 2001 was called "Skyros in Thailand" and the ethos was the same as the one we had experienced on Skyros Island in Greece.

We flew to Bangkok, spending a night there and managing to do a little sightseeing next morning before travelling by coach to the coast and boarding a boat to the island of Ko Samet, which was the venue for the course. It was a beautiful island. We spent the first day, before the course got underway, getting to know some of the other course participants and exploring the island a little. There were a number of courses on offer and I signed up to do another one led by Ari Badanes; it was two years since I had undertaken my Louise Hay training and I wanted to take further steps along my own inner journey. However, it was not to be.

The next day, Tuesday January 16th, at seven o'clock in the evening after showering and changing, I left the room I shared with Marigold to meet a couple of other women who had invited me to their room for a Gin and Tonic before dinner. They had bought some Duty-Free Gin at the airport and as I was very partial to a G&T I accepted readily. Marigold was not so keen so I went on my own.

**With Marigold in Bangkok
Monday January 15th, 2001**

All the rooms were set in a rain forest on a hillside and ours was quite high up; they were on built on stilts and spaced apart in single wooden structures over a fair distance. Consequently there were a number of long wooden staircases dotted around the complex to enable access between each building. It was just getting dark as I approached the first of these staircases leading downwards and I found it difficult to see my way. I reached out with my foot towards the top step and I felt as though I had stepped on something that wasn't there. I was tumbling through the darkness in slow motion. The glass that I had in my hand ready for the Gin and Tonic went flying high before shattering into pieces on the ground as the glass and I both crashed at the bottom of the steps. I was in a heap and I knew at once that it was impossible for me to get up. My left ankle was shattered as well as the glass and I was in great pain. In a state of shock I called out weakly for help. I couldn't see anyone and I thought it was doubtful that I could be seen, but people gradually appeared out of the darkness and came to my assistance. As they gathered around me they said encouragingly that maybe it was just a sprain but I knew it was more than that. I was in shock and sweating profusely. Someone gave me some Bach Rescue Remedy which helped to cool my temperature. After support had been mustered from the local Thai people I was carried on a makeshift stretcher down hundreds more steps to the water's edge and I was put on a speedboat and taken back to the mainland, accompanied by Marigold and Jane, the course host. Reaching the mainland coast I was carefully lifted up over the top of the harbour wall (Marigold said later that she was afraid they were going to drop me in the water) and I was placed in the back of an open truck. We were driven twenty miles to the hospital in Bangkok along the road down which we had travelled by coach two days previously. Lying there in the truck as it bumped along the road I looked along my body towards my left foot and saw it lying at a very strange angle.

  Arriving at Bumrungrad Hospital on the outskirts of Bangkok I was pushed on a trolley to the X-ray room. After inspecting my travel insurance document (which some thoughtful person had run back to my room to fetch before I was carried off the island) the doctors agreed to treat me and went ahead with the X-rays. The damage was assessed and I was told I would need an operation. At this I panicked. I had imagined that I would simply need to have my ankle set in plaster while it mended. The doctor told me that I had broken my ankle badly in three places and the bones would need to be realigned and screwed together. I had never broken a bone nor had any kind of operation in my life. In fact I had had very little to do with hospitals apart from giving birth to my children in them. I was very scared and my blood pressure was going sky high. Because of this I was told it would not be safe to give me a general anaesthetic but instead I would be given an epidural which would take away all sensation in my body from the waist down. I was slightly relieved at this as I had always dreaded the thought of being "put under".

I was given strong pain killers and wheeled into a very large private room to wait for a few hours until the operation could take place. Two extra beds were brought into the room for Marigold and Jane. I was grateful for their company. The three of us lay there dozing until 1.00am when the door opened and I was wheeled along to the operating theatre. It all seemed so unreal and I was in a daze. I was given the epidural and as I lay on the operating table I was told to put my arms out at right angles to my body so they could be strapped down. I felt like Jesus on the cross. I started to shake and shiver with fear. The anaesthetist at my side said in English, "Are you cold?" and I replied, "No I'm scared!" I remained conscious throughout the operation but I could see and feel nothing of what the surgeon was doing. My ears however, were attuned to every sound. First there was the beeping of the heart monitor that I was familiar with from TV hospital dramas. I kept thinking that as long as I could still hear that "beep, beep, beep", I would know that I was still alive! Then as the surgeon began the serious work of repairing my ankle I could hear other sounds, - the grating noise of the saw going back and forth as it cut into my bone, then the loud screechy sound as each of the six screws was being inserted into my ankle and tightened up. My ankle was then bound up in pink bandage and I was put in the recovery room while sensation gradually began to restore itself to my lower half and the pain began. I was given more pain killers and wheeled back to my room; Marigold and Jane were there to greet me and we slept for a few hours. The next day they returned to the island and I remained in the hospital for the next week. This was not how I expected to be spending my personal development holiday in Thailand.

During that week the nurses asked me what I would like to eat while I was there, - American food or Thai food. I didn't relish the idea of a diet of burgers and chips so I opted for Thai food. For the next seven days I lived on the kind of meals which I might have ordered in a Thai restaurant in England. For breakfast, lunch and dinner I was fed a diet of boiled rice, green curry, noodles, delicately cooked chicken and fish flavoured with lime leaves, coconut milk and lemon grass and always accompanied by a spicy soup. It wasn't until some years later that I could summon up enough enthusiasm to go to a restaurant for a Thai meal again.

While in the hospital I was visited by Ari Badanes who wryly joked that I would do anything to get out of one of his challenging personal development courses! I was grateful for his visit and sent a note back with him to the holidaymakers I had left behind expressing some degree of positivity about my situation. I was profoundly grateful that I hadn't broken my back. I was also grateful for the television in my hospital room which broadcast a few English films. The only time during that week that I was really able to forget my situation was when I watched "Notting Hill". It has been a favourite ever since. Apart from that film there was one other moment on the television that I remember and it was so significant that I wrote it down immediately. On Saturday January 20th, at 1.45pm local time, there was an advertisement for holidays in Thailand. The slogan shouted at me as it seemed so ironic:

"It's amazing what a visit to Thailand can do for life!"

The response I receive from most people when I relate the story of my accident is one of horror; they expect me to relate tales of a grimy hospital, primitive conditions and poor treatment. On the contrary, it was a state-of-the-art private hospital, complete with a McDonald's restaurant, a Starbucks coffee bar and every modern facility. The reception area was reminiscent of a five star hotel. I received excellent treatment and although I have been told it differed a little from standard practice in the UK, (the six screws had been inserted without a metal plate) the consultants back in Reading told me that the Thai surgeon had done a good job. I discovered much later that this hospital was a leading destination for what is known as "medical tourism", to which visitors from other countries travel for the specific purpose of undergoing cosmetic procedures such as liposuction. This was the source of much amusement for my colleagues when I eventually returned to work!

I remained in hospital staring at the four walls of my room and looking through the window to the bleak, uninspiring view beyond until I was booked on to a flight back to England, "repatriated" as my insurance company called it. I was seated in business class for the long-haul flight because of the leg room I needed (the first time I had ever had an upgrade) and was very lucky to be sitting next to a young Irish woman called Roísín. She was not only a nurse but she had also had the same operation some years previously. She showed me the scars on both sides of her ankle (the left ankle in her case too!) and later, after my bandages had been removed I discovered that my scars were in exactly the same positions as hers. I was still in a state of subdued shock during that flight and Roísín was an extremely supportive presence; she was very reassuring about my future recovery. This was surely a wonderful instance of synchronicity.

Arriving at Heathrow I was pleased to be met by airport staff waiting for me with a wheelchair and to be told that transport had been arranged for the onward journey to Reading. At the airport I gained two small insights into what life can be like as a person with a disability. The first was while going through passport control. I handed up my passport from my wheelchair but I was ignored. It was the person pushing me with whom the interaction took place; I had become a nobody.

The other insight happened just after this when I needed the toilet. On the plane I had managed with difficulty to negotiate the short distance to the toilet on crutches but it was such a struggle that I couldn't face it a second time. Consequently I was very keen to find a toilet when I arrived at Heathrow after the thirteen-hour flight! I was pushed in my wheelchair to the disabled toilet and found it was engaged. We waited for a very long time and could hear the sounds of the wash basin being used inside. Eventually a young man emerged looking beautifully clean and coiffed, without any apparent disability or indeed any sign of embarrassment. I was astonished and from then on it has become a point of honour with me to make sure that any disabled toilet is always left vacant in case it is needed in a hurry by someone who really is disabled.

My son and daughter were at my home to greet me on my return to Reading on that cold, wet Monday morning in January.

They told me later that my hair had been sticking up and I looked as though I were still in shock. They took me immediately to see my own doctor. He sent me to the Royal Berkshire Hospital to have my leg put in plaster as it was still wrapped in the pink bandages which had been applied after the operation a week previously. I was given a pair of crutches to replace the ones I had been given in Thailand, which were the kind which fitted under the arms. These were not a comfortable design and so were replaced with forearm crutches. I coped with the challenge of living on my own and being unable to go out by ordering my weekly groceries on line and engaging cleaners to do the general housework. My son arranged to hire a wheelchair for me from the Red Cross and I was grateful to my sister who came over regularly to drive me to my hospital appointments. I could manage. With Marigold's help I even organised a little party for some of the holiday people who lived within travelling distance and we ate some spicy Thai food!

I was off sick from work for the next twelve weeks. I now felt the need to occupy my enforced three months at home with some meaningful activity. This felt like an opportunity. I had a book sitting on my bookshelves which I had bought some years earlier and which I had been meaning to read for some time but I had let pressure of work and general life get in the way. It was "The Artist's Way" by Julia Cameron. It contained a twelve week course on creativity and I now had twelve weeks ahead of me and nothing much to do. Another piece of synchronicity, I thought. I followed the course with dedication and gusto. One of the main tasks was to write "Morning Pages". These were three pages of A4 which were to be written in longhand every day before doing anything else. They did not have to be perfect prose; they were meant simply to enable expression of any thoughts, desires, feelings, wishes or even nonsense that the writer needed to "get out". It is a way of clearing out all the little bits of residue which can clog up our minds and it can be extraordinarily therapeutic. Sometimes I didn't want to do it and this resistance is apparently quite common. However I persevered and felt quite triumphant at the end.

There are those who think that everything which happens to us does so for a reason. I prefer to see things which happen to us as opportunities: opportunities to learn, to grow, to deepen our understanding and to change. I would not say that my accident happened in order for me to have three months off work to pursue the course outlined in "The Artist's Way" but it did provide me with some time out and the opportunity to use this time to reflect.

Soon after returning to work following my three months' absence I booked a week's holiday for myself by the sea in Devon. I wanted further time to convalesce and reflect. UNISON owned a holiday centre at Croyde Bay near Barnstaple and it was the ideal place. My company car had been upgraded to an automatic because I could no longer use my left foot to operate the clutch and I drove from Reading along the M4, M5 and the North Devon link road (the A361) to Croyde Bay feeling in charge of my own destiny once again. I was still using a stick to support me while walking and it took me a while each day to walk the short distance to the beach but it was a very peaceful spot and I felt I had regained some of my previous independence. Seven years later I would become very familiar with the route to North Devon, but for quite a different reason.

As a result of my injury I sustained some permanent damage. The six screws which were inserted into my ankle are still there and will remain there forever. I have and shall always have restricted movement in my left ankle, permanent swelling of the joint and continual recurrent pain. After undergoing a course of physiotherapy when I came off the crutches I was told that no more could be done for me: I had been diagnosed with osteoarthritis in that ankle. I can no longer wear shoes with even the tiniest heel as it is too painful. Going down steps of any kind present a bit of a challenge as I always need to hold on to a rail.

My friends told me that I should sue the holiday company. I resisted their suggestion as I felt some kind of (misplaced?) loyalty to Skyros, having been on three Skyros holidays previously and I had enjoyed them. Eventually however, when I realised that the pain in my ankle was not going away I was persuaded to pursue a claim for compensation. I had after all sustained a severe injury through no fault of my own, suffered a great deal of shock and pain and would reap the consequences for the rest of my life. One of the holidaymakers had taken photographs of the steps where I'd had my accident; the bad state of disrepair was quite evident as was the broken light at the top. This formed a valuable part of the evidence and there was no problem in Skyros' insurance company admitting liability from the start; they agreed that the wooden steps were uneven and in need of repairing and the lights at the top and bottom had not been working. The company's health and safety arrangements were severely lacking.

Three years later I received a reasonable amount of money as compensation for all my suffering which I felt was fair. I am thankful that my accident did not result in any worse injury. I was lucky not to have broken my back and have constantly appreciated the fact that although I can no longer run I am still able to walk and even to dance. For that I am truly grateful.

Chapter 19

My father speaks to me again

"Older and wiser voices can help you find the right path, if you are only willing to listen."
Jimmy Buffett

The year following my accident I received another bolt from the blue. This time it was in the form of a letter from the South East Regional Office of the NUT and it landed on my doormat one morning in November 2002 just before I left for work. It read:

"Dear Mrs Evans,

We have received a letter (copy enclosed) from Radovan Helt in the Czech Republic. As you can see from the letter Mr Helt is trying to locate a Jeannie Evans who lives in Earley who was a teacher. We have checked our database and your name came up. As you are listed on the computer as having left the profession I am not sure if this letter will reach you safely.

If you are Wing Commander Benjamin's daughter I have a sealed envelope for you from Radovan Helt. If you could please contact me to confirm your details I will then forward the envelope to you.

Yours sincerely,
Bridget Ashplant,
Prof Admin Assistant"

I had never heard of this man called Radovan Helt whom they said was trying to trace me. The enclosed letter that he had written to the NUT gave me more information and read as follows:

"*Dear Sirs,*

I am turning to you with a request. I am seeking any informations and photos of a British hero – Wing Commander Eric Arthur Benjamin DSO, DFC, /RAF VR/ who died on 19th Feb. 1945, being killed in action. I found out that one of his daughters has been a Schoolteacher. Her name is Jeannie Evans and I have got an information she lives in Earley near Reading in Oxfordshire.

My English friend and a former member of RAF, John West of Steyning contacted you by telephone for some more information about Mrs. Evans but there is Data Protection Act there and he could not receive any informations plus.

Please, give my letter /as an enclosure/ to hands of Mrs. Jeannie Evans.

Thank you for your kind help in advance and I am looking forward to result of my several years long research. Best wishes.....

"*Lest we forget!*"
Yours sincerely,
Radovan H E L T

Member of RAF Bomber Command Assn No 11912 and owner of Museum and Exposition 'Air war over Most = Brux' "

This I found astounding. A man who was totally unknown to me had been searching for me for many years and had finally tracked me down. What makes his search and his success so remarkable is the "coincidence" involved in his having an English friend, a former member of the RAF, who lived in the Sussex town of Steyning where my mother had lived and whom she must have known. And somehow this man, a Mr John West, (another name which meant nothing to me) had made the connection between my mother and the Jeannie Evans that Radovan Helt was trying to find. I suppose that she must have spoken about me to John West and he had not only remembered my name but also that I was a teacher and somehow knew that I lived in a place called Earley on the outskirts of Reading! This was remarkable as it was now eleven years after my mother's death and at that time I had still been living in Sevenoaks.

After reading these two bombshell-letters I could not drive to work quickly enough. As soon as I arrived in my office I phoned the NUT and told them that I was indeed the person they were looking for, even though I now had a different name, which was of course the name of my father. The woman in the NUT office seemed very happy to play her part in this detective story and I waited impatiently for her to send the sealed envelope addressed to me which Radovan Helt had enclosed with his letter to the NUT. What did this man want? Once again I fantasised that my father was trying to contact me.

The third letter and the final piece of this particular jigsaw arrived a few days later enclosed in the sealed envelope, meant for my eyes only. It read:

"Dear Mrs. Evans,

I am turning to you by this way through the NUT because I do not know your address.

I am the owner of Museum and Exposition "Air War over Most = Brux" and I am seeking for details of British raid on Brux on 16/17 January 1945. I found out that the Master Bomber /Main Controller/ of this the most successful allied raid on Brux Oil Industry was your Father, Eric Arthur Benjamin DSO, DFC for my Museum for several years already.

I would be very pleased if you could give me anything in touch with your Father. And his photo will be very welcomed.

Thanks of your Father and his very accuracy work over Brux. O/I was German Oil Industry here almost destroyed with minimum of losses of civilians.

I will be looking forward to your any answer. Thank you for your kind help in advance.

Best wishes, Radovan Helt."

Now at last I had some answers. Radovan Helt owned a museum in the Czech Republic and was researching a British raid which had taken place over Brux, (the German name for the town of Most which was restored to Czechoslovakia after the war). My father had apparently led the raid on the Brux oil industry just a month before he was killed and Mr Helt obviously had a great regard for him and was seeking more information about him. Once again I was left open-mouthed as I read this letter. I had not expected to receive a letter of thanks for my father's heroism fifty-seven years after his death! My father's past life seemed to have a habit of inserting itself into my present life.

A response was clearly necessary and over the next few months and years a dialogue ensued between me and Mr Helt as I did my best to supply answers to his continuing questions. I was greatly helped in this task by the fact that my sister was at that time in a relationship with a man who had a great interest in the aircraft of the Second World War. On behalf of my sister he carried out some research into our father's war record which brought to light much information of which we were only dimly aware. Before he and my sister split up he had begun to put together a record of my father's life which he entitled "The Bride Wore Green". This was taken from a headline in the "Sunday Pictorial" on Sunday December 3rd 1939, the day my parents got married.

The story of my parents' wedding day is one you couldn't make up! They had been courting for nearly two years and the onset of war in 1939 meant that they decided to get married sooner than they had planned. War had broken out on September 3rd and they got married exactly three months later. My mother had often told me and Sally how she wasn't interested in the details of the wedding, she simply wanted to be married to the man she loved so much. Consequently she chose a green dress, which set off her beautiful auburn hair. She was not at all bothered with choosing a conventional white one. The symbolism of a white dress was not an issue; she was definitely a virgin as can be seen from her own account of spending a night with Eric some time before their wedding. Neither was she concerned with any superstitious notions of wearing green which the newspapers later picked up.

On the expected morning of the wedding, which had been set for Saturday December 2nd, one of my mother's younger sisters, my Auntie Winnie, who was to have been a bridesmaid, was suddenly taken ill and rushed to hospital with peritonitis. This was a very serious illness and she had to undergo an operation. However, once it became clear that she was out of danger, my parents were urged to go ahead with the wedding and everyone assembled at the church. Bride, groom and guests were all there, everyone in fact, except the registrar. The ceremony could not go ahead without him as the wedding was taking place in a Catholic church and the presence of a registrar was necessary in order to fulfil the legal function. After waiting in vain for a couple of hours everyone realised that he was not going to turn up. Two of the guests went in search of him, hoping that the wedding could still take place that day but it transpired that the registrar had made a mistake about the date and he could not be found.

Since the reception had already been prepared back at my mother's parents' house they decided to go ahead with the celebrations despite no wedding having taken place. So the wedding cake was cut, the "bride and groom" were toasted and my mother spent that night back at her parental home without my father. Not to be deterred, my parents got married the following day instead. I have no idea how the national press got hold of the story but there in a double page spread of the Sunday Pictorial and other newspapers was a photograph of my mother and father cutting their wedding cake and "celebrating" the marriage which had not yet taken place. There is a photograph in the family album of a car with a placard tied to the front of its bonnet; it reads "The Bride in Green – What Happened". The newspaper made much of the superstition that the colour green worn on a wedding day would bring bad luck, and with hindsight this was to prove not to be without foundation.

My mother told me and my sister many years later that as a consequence of the wedding having been postponed by a day my mother's period had arrived and consequently their marriage was not consummated on their wedding night. This was spent in a rather old-fashioned hotel and most of the other guests were rather elderly. My mother told us that she could feel them all staring at her and her new husband when they came down to breakfast the following morning and she was somewhat amused to think that they didn't know that she was in fact still a virgin!

As well as providing revelations about our parents' wedding day (although not all of it was new to us) my sister's then partner also made another wonderful discovery. When Sally and I were growing up we had often been told the story of how my father had appeared on a Pathé newsreel in the cinema in 1943. Apart from newspapers this was how the public got its news in the days prior to television: once a week in the cinema, screened before the main feature film. My father had led an important and successful air raid over Berlin; he was interviewed on camera for the news and this was shown in cinemas throughout the country. The story was part of our family history and there is even a photograph in the family album taken from the film footage, which shows my father in the forefront of the picture. I was very familiar with this photograph. My Auntie Winnie (who recovered fully from her peritonitis and lived until the age of eighty-six) had often told us about how proud she had been when she saw my father on the cinema news. She said she wanted to stand up and shout to the whole audience, "That's my brother-in-law!"

In his research my sister's ex-partner had discovered a video of that very piece of cinema footage. It was included in a documentary called "Operation Failed to Return", distributed by

Bygone Films, which shows the unveiling in 1989 at RAF Skellingthorpe near Lincoln, of a memorial to those who died in the night skies over Nazi Germany. The video includes what it says is the only wartime newsreel taken at Skellingthorpe. The film clip is entitled "Berlin Raiders", and in it my father speaks about his experience as a member of Bomber Command leading a raid over Berlin and dropping bombs from a Lancaster. He talks about it with huge modesty and without triumphancy but with an amazing degree of concern and empathy for those on whom the bombs were falling. (He had been a pacifist before war broke out and had only taken flying lessons so that he could earn some extra money to get married.)

**My father on Pathé newsreel
November 1943**

I first saw the video containing this piece of newsreel in 1994. My sister and her partner had come to visit for the day. They had already watched the clip and wanted to show it to me. I could sense that Sally was particularly interested to see my reaction and I felt her watching my face as we played the video on my television. I was very self-conscious and kept my deepest reaction until they had left. Then I wept. For the first time in my conscious memory I had seen my father moving and had heard him speaking. There he was, alive on camera. I was fifty-one years old and there was my father in his early twenties, looking as handsome as he must have done to my mother all those years ago. If only she had not been killed three years earlier; she would have been amazed to see this.

That same afternoon we indulged ourselves in a cloud nostalgia and began reading some of the many wonderful love letters that my father had written to my mother. Sally and I had discovered them while clearing out my mother's bungalow after her death. They were tied up with ribbon and stacked in a shoe box at the back of her wardrobe, each letter having been carefully re-inserted into its envelope. We had read some of them at that time but after seeing my father on my television screen they had an added freshness. It was a poignant few hours. The most touching moment of all for me was to read again the poem which my father had written to me before my birth:

To Jeannie

15.12.42.

Let us Prepare.
Beyond the far horizon, slowly, creeps
A new beginning of a life to be,
So let us, while the unborn baby sleeps,
Prepare a path in God; - and let us see
That all its infant fears and childish woes
Are banished from its troubled mind; our eye -
    Our parent eye - must watch and check these foes
In youth and never let our baby cry
For want of love and guidance or a kind

And understanding friend; - for out of love
And kindness grows a stronger will, - a mind
More resolute to face, with God above,
The daily trials of this life on earth.
Prepare us, now, O God, for this new birth.

20.7.43.

Before its baby eyelids open to a scarred
And shattered world; before those precious
Eardrums vibrate to the wicked
Blare of battle; before this contaminated
Air fans those tiny nostrils and minute
Lungs expand to inhale its wickedness;
Before we hear a cry from pure, virgin lips
And infant arms reach out to resist
These daily enemies;
    - before all this, - let us pray.
Let us pray for the blessing of God, so
That our little one will have the strength
To fight all manner of evil which
Comes its way.

17.8.43.

On this day - in the morning - she came into
The world -
                Jeannie.

                      We give thanks
To God for this happy deliverance – there
Was never a greater day.

Chapter 20

Another change of direction and a visit to my father

"If you never did you should. These things are fun and fun is good."
Dr. Seuss

After my foray into national politics and my subsequent realisation that there are other ways of changing the world, I was still learning that change continues to happen regardless of any plans I may make. Even though I had now decided on a different course of action from politics and was heading in the direction of personal development training the Universe still had other ideas in store.

Having had some reasonable success in running personal development courses based on the work of Louise Hay, I wanted to add further strings to my bow so I enrolled on a year-long course which led to my gaining a qualification as an NLP Practitioner. NLP stands for Neuro-Linguistic Programming, which is a less than helpful title. One definition of it is "the study of the structure of subjective experience". It looks at the underlying structures of the skills, behaviour and experiences of excellence in human behaviour and it can be used to assist people in using these structures effectively. It has been successfully applied to the fields of business, sport, therapy, education and the performing arts. My course took place at weekends while I was still working full-time for UNISON and I found it very enjoyable as well as being very compatible with the philosophy of Louise Hay.

I experienced two memorable transformations during my training. First I managed to grow my bitten fingernails, a habit which I had had ever since I could remember. My mother had always included a little manicure set or a small bottle of nail hardener in my birthday and Christmas presents in an effort to help me overcome the habit but nothing had worked, so this was a major achievement. Secondly I overcame my phobia of using a lift. Ever since I had been stuck in a lift (albeit briefly) at the age of twelve I had been daunted by the prospect of entering one, to the extent that I would walk up ten, eleven or twelve flights of stairs to avoid doing so. Although I could manage to steel myself enough to enter a lift if I was accompanied by someone else it was becoming increasingly problematic as I ventured forth into wider arenas and so I felt a huge satisfaction and liberation once this fear had been lifted.

As I approached my sixtieth birthday in 2003 I decided to make the move into my third "career". I had been a teacher for twenty-one years and a trade union official for ten years. My new plan was to develop my fledgling personal development courses into a full-blown thriving business. The retirement age for UNISON employees was sixty-five but I reviewed my finances and decided I could afford to leave my full-time employment at the age of sixty-one. Before then however, I approached my employer to ask for funding to undertake further training in NLP so that I could become a Master Practitioner. I was delighted that they agreed to this and a few months before I left UNISON I had become a fully qualified NLP Master Practitioner. At a subsequent Louise Hay Teachers' reunion I told the story of how I had finally gained my wish to become an MP, - not a Member of Parliament but a Master Practitioner. Be careful what you wish for; the Universe may interpret it differently!

I was leaving my job but I resisted using the word "retirement" as to me that word seemed to imply that I would be taking a back seat in life and this was far from my intention. I simply told people that I was leaving UNISON to start my own business. Although this was true I think that my real resistance to the word "retirement" was based on a fear that it made me sound like an old person!

So at 9.00am on Wednesday September 1st, 2004 I was sitting up in bed on the first day of my "retirement" with a cup of tea in hand, contemplating my new life and surrounded by lots of holiday brochures. I had also made another decision. Before starting my business in earnest I would take time out until the end of the year and enjoy myself. I regarded this as my well-deserved playtime. I would put off running my courses and doing one-to-one coaching until the New Year and in the meantime I would indulge in some fun activities. I joined a singing class. I enjoyed singing and had taken a course a couple of years previously at an evening class at Reading University called "Singing from Scratch". It had interested the local television company who came along to film us on the first and last nights of the course. They picked out me and two others to interview in our workplaces. Of course they could not resist a pun about "singing in Unison"!

As well as taking singing lessons, a week into this self-designated playtime period I also bought a piano. I had gone in to a specialist music shop in Reading to buy some classical CDs as a birthday present for my son and I came out with the CDs in my bag and a piano on order! Simply on a whim! I had taken piano lessons as a child and had progressed no further than the Grade One exam which I had failed at the age of twelve. This had always rankled with me as I was not used to failing and I now wanted to have another go. The piano was delivered to my house on the following Friday. I had not even touched any of the piano keys while in the shop, not wanting to parade my ineptitude! I realised I would need to have more lessons if I were to justify spending £1,950 on a whim. A colleague recommended a local teacher. He was a very patient and kind man and I did make some progress. Eventually I reached a level which he told me was past Grade 1 and halfway towards Grade 2. (I had told him I didn't want the stress of actually taking an exam.) I had achieved my objective; I had overcome my earlier failure! As well as singing and playing the piano I went to dancing classes. I had already been going to Ceroc (a kind of jive) for a few years and I loved it. I also took up salsa dancing, which was something else I enjoyed very much.

During this playtime period thoughts of the recently discovered connections with my past were ever present in my mind and so in December of that year Sally and I went to visit our father's grave in Berlin. He was buried in the Commonwealth War Graves Commission Cemetery. Our mother had visited it once in 1987, accompanied by Fred and financed by a Royal British Legion scheme to help war widows travel abroad to their husbands' graves. However, Sally and I had never been there and as my sister was approaching her sixtieth birthday this seemed an auspicious time to go. It felt like a pilgrimage. This was the first time my sister and I had ever been away together and we booked three nights at a luxury hotel near the Brandenburg Gate.

The day after our arrival we took a taxi to the cemetery which was situated to the west of the city centre in the district of Charlottenburg. (I had named my daughter Charlotte quite unaware that this was the name of the area where her grandfather was buried.) The taxi driver kindly offered to wait while we paid our respects. It was a quiet place with a serene atmosphere, very distant from the bustle of Berlin city centre. We walked up and down the rows and rows of white headstones for some minutes until we found the number we were looking for: 1. Z. 13. There it was, one white headstone among so many others, but this one had our father's name on it:

WING COMMANDER
E.A. BENJAMIN. DFC. & BAR
PILOT
ROYAL AIR FORCE
20TH FEBRUARY 1945 AGE 25

It was a lump-in-the-throat moment. There he was lying under the earth of the country he had helped to defeat, the country over which he had dropped many bombs and where he had met his death. Our father's remains had lain there for fifty-nine years, while Sally and I had been growing up, earning a living, getting married, having children and getting divorced. All those Fridays.

Something we hadn't known about until we saw the grave was the wording inscribed at the bottom of the headstone. It read: "Until we meet again, Betty, Jeannie and Sally". "Jeannie" was spelled as "Jeanne", which led me to think that the inscription was there at the request of Nana, my maternal grandmother, as she had always spelled my name like that on the birthday cards she had sent me during my childhood! Perhaps that was why as a child and teenager I had always felt a strong identification with Joan of Arc, (Jeanne d'Arc). I'm not sure.

**At my father's grave
December 2004**

We laid the flowers which we had bought from a local market and stood together in silent contemplation for a while. We shed a few tears there in the cemetery but not a lot as most of them had been shed privately in our hotel rooms during the previous evening in anticipation of this moment. We had accomplished our mission. It had been a difficult one but a very worthwhile one.

Chapter 21

I Can Do It!

"You are the power in your world! You get to have whatever you choose to think!"
Louise L. Hay

A month before that visit to my father's grave I had received an email from a friend, another Louise Hay teacher, saying she was interested in attending a conference in April of the following year at which Louise Hay would be the keynote speaker. The conference, called "I Can Do It!", was to take place not in England but in Las Vegas! She asked if I would like to go too, and although it was a big decision it didn't take me long to say yes. I bought my conference tickets and committed myself. Then my plans really began to take shape. If I was going to fly all that way I would make good use of it and see more of the west coast of America than just Las Vegas. More importantly, I decided to go and visit my father's relatives in Canada whom I had never met and whose existence I had only discovered a few years previously! I contacted my father's cousin Frances and she was delighted.

So my plans for pursuing my personal development business in earnest were once more put on hold while I spent the early part of 2005 preparing my itinerary and making arrangements for my transatlantic visit to Frances and her sister Eunice. I had never done anything as adventurous as this before, to travel such a long distance on my own, arrange it all myself, and go and see people I had never met before. I was both excited and nervous. I was certainly feeling the fear and doing it anyway! I went into a travel agent's in Reading where I sat down and outlined my plans.

My itinerary would be as follows: San Francisco, Vancouver Island, Los Angeles, Las Vegas. And so it was that on Monday April 4th, 2005, with much trepidation, I set out on my journey from Heathrow to San Francisco. During the flight I chatted to the woman sitting next to me who was travelling with her husband and she commented that I was very brave to do such a journey on my own. I agreed with her! I felt both brave and exhilarated. I was on the brink of a tremendous experience, one that I could never have imagined undertaking in those dark days of fear and unhappiness as my marriage was crumbling.

Arriving in the USA after the eleven hour flight I was transported to my hotel in a white stretch limo, the first of many in which I was to travel during the next few weeks. I felt ecstatic as I checked in to my hotel on Fisherman's Wharf. Although I was tired and suffering from jet lag I couldn't wait to start exploring my immediate surroundings. I found the San Francisco Bay area a very friendly place and easy to wander around. I booked myself on to an organised tour of the city for the following morning and then strolled on to the famous Pier 39 where I stood and watched dozens of sea lions flopping around on rafts and making very loud honking noises. The local story was that they had arrived in the bay after the 1989 earthquake and decided to stay, but this has not been verified. I found a lovely restaurant on the pier called "Chic's" and enjoyed the first meal of my West Coast adventure, fresh fish and chips with a glass of Sauvignon Blanc. Having been awake nearly twenty-four hours I walked back to my hotel somewhat dizzily. I awoke the next morning feeling more than ready for all the new experiences that awaited me.

Since most hotels in America are supplied on a room-only basis I needed to find somewhere to have breakfast before going on the city tour I had booked. I found a diner called "The International House of Pancakes" and it lived up to its name. I ordered two pancakes stuffed with bacon and cheese and they came with extra buttermilk pancakes topped with cream cheese! I could see I was going to have to be careful about my cholesterol intake over the next few weeks.

My coach tour took me to all the famous sights of the city, including of course the Golden Gate Bridge, and I continued my tour with a cruise around the bay which took me underneath that iconic bridge as well as around the island of Alcatraz with its notorious, now abandoned prison. Having got my bearings, the following day I made my way around the city independently, travelling on the famous Cable Car into the downtown area, having a coffee in Union Square and walking back through Chinatown. I couldn't resist calling into the City Lights Bookstore, home of the Beat Generation of the 1950s, and having a browse there before returning to Fisherman's Wharf. On the famous Pier 39 I had another meal of fish and chips and a couple of glasses of wine and watched the seals again as they floundered around just below. Walking back to my hotel feeling slightly tipsy I bought a couple of sleeveless fleeces emblazoned with the Golden Gate logo. I had thoroughly enjoyed this first leg of my tailor-made tour and was finding it easy to get around on my own. My anxieties were rapidly dissipating.

At the start of my West Coast adventure
Golden Gate Bridge, San Francisco
April 2005

After three nights in San Francisco I prepared for the internal flight north to Vancouver. As I checked in my baggage at San Francisco airport a friendly male baggage attendant said in a kindly way, "Oh dear, are you all on your lonesome?" and I proudly replied, "Yes and loving it!" Arriving at Vancouver I was met as arranged by Eunice, one of my father's cousins, and her husband Harry who were both about ten years older than me. We had only each other's photos to go on but we recognised each other instantly.

Harry drove us to the huge British Columbia car ferry which carried us across the Strait of Georgia to Vancouver Island. Eunice had prepared a picnic which we ate on the ferry while we started to get to know each other. We continued to the north of the island, heading for the town of Courtenay in the Comox Valley where Eunice's sister Frances lived with her husband Mark. This was another three hours' drive so by the time we arrived we were beginning to get to know one another quite well.

Frances was extremely welcoming and because she and I had been in frequent contact by telephone and letter I felt I already knew her. She had carried out a great deal of research into the Benjamin family history and the next morning she produced files bulging with photographs, letters and copies of the family tree which she spread out over her kitchen table. She showed me letters that my father had written to his aunt and uncle in Canada when he was nineteen years old and she provided the information about the plane crash which had had such a devastating effect on François' life. While I was perusing all these fascinating documents the funeral of Pope John-Paul 2nd was taking place in Rome on Friday April 8th and the marriage of Prince Charles to Camilla Parker-Bowles was happening on the following day. I was amused by the fact that my Canadian cousins were much more interested in both events than I was. They were neither Catholics nor UK subjects and yet they watched the coverage of these events on television with a keen interest.

During the next few days I was treated as an honoured guest. Frances' husband Mark took me, Eunice and Harry on a tour around the area, which included a visit to the local museum where I learned something about the "First Nation" peoples, (I learned not to call them Indians) and I saw authentic "Totem Poles" which were situated all around the neighbourhood. Meanwhile Frances was at home preparing a wonderful meal and that evening a large family gathering took place in my honour. Frances and Mark's children and grandchildren had all been invited and I felt like royalty as I was introduced to everyone. It was a very special occasion. When I said goodbye to Frances and Mark a few days later I was quite tearful.

**Family gathering of my "new" Canadian relatives
(L to R Back Row: Harry, Eunice, Jacqueline, Margaret, Frances, Richard, Tom; Front Row: Mark, Mackenzie, Kim)
Vancouver Island
April 2005**

Eunice and Harry drove me back down to the south of the island where we spent a couple of days in Victoria, the island's capital. I was very impressed with the sight of the floodlit

Parliament building at night and even more impressed when we went into the museum and saw the wonderfully decorated yellow Rolls-Royce which had belonged to John Lennon. I had no idea that it was there in Victoria. We returned to the mainland on the British Columbia car ferry and found our way to the airport; this was the first time I had seen a satellite navigation system in action and I was impressed. Eunice and Harry had looked after me every inch of the way and I was very grateful for all their kindness. As the three of us waited at Vancouver airport for me to check in to my flight there was a further surprise in store for me. Another of my Canadian relatives, Frances' and Eunice's nephew Darryl, had made a special journey to come and see me before I left Canada. We only had a matter of minutes together but he bought me a sandwich and we had a little time to make each other's acquaintance. I was very touched by the effort he had made to meet me. Saying goodbye to the three of them (again somewhat tearfully) I boarded my flight to Los Angeles for the next leg of my journey and in a short time I was back in the USA once again.

With Eunice and Harry in front of John Lennon's Rolls-Royce Royal BC Museum, Victoria, Vancouver Island April 2005

Once more I was whisked in a stretch limo from the airport (LAX as it is known) to my hotel, which was located in the Santa Monica area. As I walked in to the foyer lined with enormous palm trees I gasped at the sheer opulence of my surroundings. I had spared no expense for this trip and it was paying dividends. After a short rest in my room I came down to the lobby to meet my friend Margaret and her husband Mike as arranged. Everything was going to plan. Margaret was the friend who had first suggested that we go to the Louise Hay conference in Las Vegas and she and her husband were spending a few days further down the Californian coast in San Diego before travelling on to the conference. We had planned to meet in LA and our plans had worked - there they were! After the three of us enjoyed a meal together Margaret and I booked ourselves on a tour of Hollywood for the next morning. I was not particularly interested in films or film stars but as I was in Los Angeles of course it had to be done! We were taken on a tour around the film studios and the famous Kodak theatre where the academy awards are held, we did the "Walk of Fame", we visited the only remaining "speakeasy" and we were shown the grand houses in Beverley Hills which were homes to the rich and famous. It was a fun day out! Mike drove Margaret back down to San Diego and I spent the next couple of days on my own exploring Santa Monica and Venice Beach before leaving Los Angeles. Once again I felt very proud of myself for being so independent.

After another short internal flight I was in Las Vegas; I was not prepared for such an overwhelming experience! The airport itself appeared to be one big casino! I had booked myself into the most prestigious hotel on the Strip, the Bellagio, inspired by the Lake Como resort of Bellagio in Italy. Margaret's husband Mike had told me that if I thought the hotel in LA was grand I would be staggered when I got to Las Vegas. He was right. I had never seen anything so sumptuous in my life. It was truly another world. Everything I saw left me completely open-mouthed in admiration, from the beautiful hand-blown coloured glass flowers on the ceiling of the enormous foyer to the twenty-seven-foot high chocolate fountain which loomed large as I wandered further inside. I was by now getting used to large hotel rooms (most of them contained two double beds) but the bathroom here surpassed them all with its walk-in shower big enough for three people at one end and a king size Jacuzzi bath at the other. It entailed a lot of walking! I treated myself to room service that evening and although I only ordered a snack it arrived on a trolley complete with a white tablecloth, a rose in a vase and a silver domed food cover which was lifted with great flourish by the waiter to display my two small spring rolls!

The next morning was hot and sunny and I ventured out to explore the other hotels on the Strip. I wasn't keen on the vast casinos for which Las Vegas in renowned and which forced themselves on my attention as I entered each hotel but I was very impressed with the sheer inventiveness (and, it has to be said, the vulgarity) of it all. I hadn't really known what to expect and had not appreciated that each hotel was designed as a replica of a particular city in the world. There were three-quarter sized versions of all the famous monuments of Paris, New York, Cairo, Venice and Rome. As I walked down the famous Strip in the warm April sunshine I passed the Eiffel Tower, the Trevi Fountain and the Giza Pyramid, eventually arriving at the Venetian Hotel which was to be the venue for the Louise Hay Conference, and there I was presented with the sight of the Rialto Bridge and gondolas passing underneath! I stopped for lunch in an indoor St. Mark's Square before strolling back up the strip and by then it was getting very hot indeed.

By the time I reached The Bellagio I was ready for a siesta. However, my attention was caught by the sight of some magnificent fountains in the huge lake on the other side of the hotel. As I drew nearer I could hear the most glorious music and I realised that the fountain display was moving in time with the music, with the water swaying from side to side and leaping to enormous heights! I was entranced and stayed listening and watching for nearly an hour. I learned that this spectacle took place at regular intervals and so I returned later to enjoy a further show as dusk was falling. As I stood there watching and listening to a range of music from Frank Sinatra to Beethoven my eyes filled with tears; this was one of the few moments of my West Coast adventure that I would love to have shared with someone else.

The main purpose of my stay in Las Vegas however, was to attend the "I Can Do It!" conference with my friend Margaret. Indeed it was the whole raison d'être for my being in America. She and I enjoyed ourselves immensely over those three days, seizing the opportunity with great gusto and taking part in workshops and seminars led by eminent speakers. The conference was opened by Louise Hay herself with the words "I'm seventy-eight and feeling great!" and she was indeed an inspirational force. Her writings had been my guiding force during the previous few years, leading me further along my path of change. They had enabled me to view problems as challenges, setbacks as opportunities and above all to see life as one delicious feast with many courses to be savoured and enjoyed. The highlight of the weekend came at a book-signing when I was lucky enough to meet her and have my photograph taken with her.

**With Louise Hay in Las Vegas
April 2005**

After the conference was over I had a couple of days to spare before I was due to fly home so I gave myself two final treats to round off my adventure. I booked a very expensive seat in the Bellagio theatre and watched a wonderful show called "O", performed by the Cirque du Soleil, which took my breath away with its magnificence. On the last morning I took a helicopter ride over the Hoover Dam and up to the Grand Canyon, enjoying a champagne breakfast there and a bird's eye view of the Las Vegas Strip on the way back!

The original impetus for my travelling to the States had been to attend the Louise Hay conference in Las Vegas and although this was a brilliant and unique event it was only one part of a much bigger life-changing experience for me. Thanks to the various unexpected interventions in my life I had been able to meet previously unknown members of my father's family and I had discovered further aspects of myself in the process, thanks to my involvement in the work of Louise Hay.

I flew back to England on Wednesday April 20th, 2005. My diary entry reads:

"I loved being independent and I found it's not difficult to travel by myself, - in fact it's easy! I also learned to take care of myself, to slow down when I was getting tired and to give myself treats – like room service. It has been a great achievement and I'm so pleased I did it."

Chapter 22

From Parliamentary Candidate to Porridge Queen

"If you don't know where you are going, you'll probably end up somewhere else."
Lewis Carroll

My visits to Berlin and Canada, connected as they were with discoveries about my father, had thrown me off course as far as my plans to start my personal development business were concerned. I had retired from UNISON early to put these plans into place but now I was losing the motivation. Where was I going now? I continued with my piano lessons, my singing and my dancing; I also had a few coaching clients coming to me for one-to-one sessions. I was doing lots of travelling, sometimes with my daughter, sometimes with various friends. Within three years of retiring not only had I visited Berlin, Canada and California, I had also been to Venice, New York, Paris, Valencia, Lisbon, Florence, Majorca, Egypt, Greece, and Cambodia. In addition I had also spent many weeks at my favourite place in southern Spain, a holiday centre which ran courses of various kinds and which had been recommended to me as an alternative to Skyros. I had been to this centre on nine different occasions since discovering it in 2003, taking part in courses on singing, dancing, meditation, tai chi and personal development.

I was doing a lot of things but I had lost my focus. I had been so sure that once I had left UNISON I would be starting my business in earnest, making a difference to people's lives, doing my bit to send out ripples in the world, but here I was, travelling to lots of countries, having lots of holidays and enjoying myself! I didn't know where I was going anymore, other than to lots of fabulous places in the world! But during the summer and autumn of 2005, after my West Coast adventure, I was beginning to feel the lack of a purpose to my life and by 2006 I was feeling it very keenly. I began devouring numerous books containing advice on finding one's true purpose but I was floundering and somewhat depressed. I had lost that initial enthusiasm for running my personal development business. I half-heartedly advertised a few courses but the Universe was responding to my lack of enthusiasm in like manner: there were no applications. I had always been at my most energetic when I was undertaking a project, organising some venture or planning a celebration and three years earlier, while I was still in full-time employment, I had given a huge party for my sixtieth birthday. I hired a beautiful venue not far from my birthplace near Stoke Poges in Buckinghamshire, I invited nearly a hundred people: family, friends and colleagues from past and present, and laid on Ceroc dancing for everyone. It was a great success and I had been in my element while preparing and planning for it. That was exactly the kind of thing that I enjoyed doing: being involved in some kind of project and seeing it to a successful conclusion.

But what was I doing with my life now? Where was I going? How could I justify my existence? I struggled with these notions for many months, hoping that I would somehow discover my purpose, whatever that might be. In the 1980s and 1990s I had been focussed on trying to get into Parliament and it had come to nought. In the last few years I had put my energy into running courses and coaching sessions with the expectation that my third career was about to take off. It hadn't. My feelings were similar to those I had experienced after the 1997 General Election: I was disappointed, dejected and demoralised. What was I to do with the rest of my life?

During the winter of 2005/2006 I experienced a taste of the depression with which many people are familiar; some call it S.A.D. syndrome, Seasonal Affective Disorder; it was totally unfamiliar to me. I was listless, unhappy and directionless. Since the mind and body are totally interconnected, it was not surprising that I also developed physical problems. I had a recurrent cough, my ears needed syringing and I started to hear a ringing in my left ear. It was tinnitus and it sent me into a state of panic. I had a few consultations at the audiology department of the Royal Berkshire Hospital and these sessions along with a few NLP processes which I practised on myself provided me with some solutions but I knew that I would need to deal with the deeper malaise that I was experiencing. As the year progressed and the weather improved I gradually shook off my low mood and I continued with my usual activities: meeting friends for lunch, going to tai chi classes, doing a few coaching sessions for clients, carrying out some freelance work for UNISON and enjoying a few more holidays. But this wasn't enough to dispel my feeling that I was going nowhere.

An idea was taking hold which had cropped up the previous year while I was on one of my holiday courses in Spain. I started to fantasise about buying a house out there and had even been to look at a few of them with the local *immobilaria* (estate agents). Maybe this was to be the purpose I needed for my life to regain its momentum. It would certainly give me something to focus on and to plan for. But to give up my home in England and to move to Spain to live permanently would be a step too far and I decided that it would be better for me to spend half a year in England and half a year in Spain. As I didn't have enough savings to buy a home in Spain outright this would mean downsizing in order to release the extra cash. I would have to sell my house in Reading and find somewhere smaller in the area. I had my house valued and began to look for a smaller house where I could live for six months of each year.

That summer I went to my usual holiday centre again for a fortnight to do two consecutive courses. The title of the second week's course was "Letting Go And Moving On"! Was it now time for me to let go of my old familiar life? Maybe it was. A member of the staff at the holiday centre wanted to sell her house and I went to look at it. This could be my opportunity. However I was still a little nervous about the idea and made no commitment.

Once again my daughter, who had been so supportive in the lead up to my divorce nineteen years earlier, offered her help. She advised me to look at the property in winter before coming to a decision and offered to accompany me on a visit there for that specific purpose. We duly flew out there later that year, on a December weekend, spending one night in a nearby hotel; it was a whistle-stop tour. The nearby market town which I knew so well and which had always been so lively and warm was now very cold and empty. The atmosphere was completely changed. Charlotte and I sat in a bar on a bitterly cold evening drinking vodka and tonic to which the barman had added a tumbler full of ice cubes! With a sudden realisation I knew that I could not live there; I would be isolated from my friends and family and this was not the solution I was seeking. It was a good lesson.

I had decided that uprooting myself to live in Spain, even on a part-year basis, was not for me but I was still determined to avoid a repeat of the depression I had experienced the previous winter. The holiday centre to which I had become so attached ran a scheme whereby they engaged a volunteer to work for three months at a time alongside the permanent paid members of staff. Just before my abortive house-buying visit to Spain in December 2006 I had applied for this volunteer post, had attended an interview and been successful. I agreed to get a qualification in first aid and I would work there as an unpaid volunteer for the first three months of 2007. I was overjoyed. I would have the opportunity of belonging to a community of like-minded people, albeit on a temporary basis and I could make some contribution to the world. I would also avoid the harshness of the English winter, for even though Spain could be cold at that time of year it had the great advantage of plenty of sunshine. I also thought that three months' "time out" would give me the opportunity to reassess my life. Somewhere at the back of my mind I imagined that I would experience a "light-bulb" moment when all would become clear and I would know what to do with the rest of my life.

The duties of the volunteer were many and varied. They included being available to the guests at all times, preparing breakfast, washing up, assisting the cook with the preparation of vegetables for lunch and dinner for up to twenty-four people, more washing up, gathering logs for the fire, lighting the fire, cleaning the fireplace, making up the weekly picnic in large rucksacks, and more washing up. If the central heating system failed it was the volunteer's job to tinker with the boiler and if guests were taken ill it was also the volunteer's job to accompany them to the *Centro de Salud* (Health Centre). In return the volunteer would be provided with free meals and accommodation, two days off a week and a week's free holiday at the end.

My two days off did not materialise and I was lucky if I got even one day off in a week as there was always the need for me to cover the duties of permanent staff while they were on leave or undergoing training courses. This meant that I was unable to have a night away as I had hoped. I was often the only "member of staff" on duty, albeit a volunteer and unpaid. It was a huge responsibility and I began to feel more and more disgruntled, not to say exhausted and eventually became ill with a peptic ulcer. I felt I was being exploited but because I was not being paid I felt I had no right to complain. What had happened to my assertiveness and my self-esteem? I had trained many women over the years in assertiveness techniques: how to say "no", how to stand up for their rights and how to state what they wanted when they were in a difficult situation. I had also represented employees who were being oppressed in the workplace; as a union representative I knew about employment law and workers' rights. If as a union rep I had encountered someone who was in a similar situation I would have gone straight to management to complain. But somehow I could not do this for myself. It was easier for me to fight battles on behalf of others than to fight my own.

During the course of those three months I did eventually manage to make a few attempts to assert myself and I gained a few concessions. As a result I even had a couple of days away in a hotel in Granada which was bliss. However, one of my abiding memories is of standing over the stove in the kitchen at 7.30am stirring a huge cauldron of porridge and feeling exhausted but still taking pride in making it as smooth as possible. Porridge was on the menu twice a week and was something the guests always looked forward to; I was rewarded with cries of delight as they came in for breakfast and tasted the results of my efforts. Many of them said it was the smoothest porridge they had ever tasted and they complimented me on my porridge-making skills. I couldn't help a wry smile as I thought that once I had been a Parliamentary Candidate and now I was the Porridge Queen! It was a humbling moment.

As a postscript to this experience it is important to mention that after my three months' "slave labour" as I called it somewhat dramatically, I submitted a detailed written report to the director of the holiday centre when I returned to England. As a result of my suggestions a number of changes were made to the duties of the volunteer and extra paid help was brought in to carry out some of the work (particularly the washing up)! So I was glad that my suffering had not been in vain; I had brought about a change for future participants in the scheme and this knowledge brought me some satisfaction. Since doing my stint as a volunteer I have been back several times as a course participant and I am pleased to say I have made my peace with the place. It remains a sanctuary for me.

Chapter 23

Another unexpected change of direction

"Life is what happens to you
while you're busy making other plans."
from "Beautiful Boy", by John Lennon

It is more than thirty years since John Lennon was killed. He would now be over seventy years old. All those Fridays had come and gone and I too would soon be approaching my seventieth year. How had I acquitted myself in those intervening years? So many plans made, so many different directions taken and so many different paths followed. Where was I going? Where am I still going?

After my three months' "work experience" in Spain in 2007 I returned to England somewhat relieved to be home but no further forward in my quest to find my "purpose". I had imagined that after my time out there I would return knowing exactly what I was going to do with the rest of my life. No such luck. There had been no "light bulb" moment. Coming back to my home in Reading I was brought down to earth with a bump. Returning from Gatwick airport in a taxi I was confronted with road works directly outside my house which were blocking the entrance; this meant that my taxi driver had to park some distance away and I had to haul my luggage the last few yards before I finally got inside the home I was so longing to reach. Once inside I heaved a huge sigh of relief before I realised how cold it was. My sister had been checking my house regularly during my absence and she had let me know only a few days previously that the heating system had been working perfectly; I now discovered that the boiler had broken down and this must have happened just prior to my return. After making arrangements to have the boiler repaired I contacted the council to ask them to remove the large concrete blocks from my entrance which were preventing me from taking my car out and they said they would be unable to do this for some days. However, when I eventually got into my car I found it had a flat battery which meant I couldn't move it anyway! Luckily a wonderful friend, Kevin, appeared at my doorstep at just the right moment and I burst into tears of relief. He helped me deal with the situation and provided me with the support, practical and emotional, which I needed just then.

After dealing with all these practical matters and returning to "normal life" I found myself floundering again. No magical metamorphosis had taken place, for as others wiser than me have noted, when you go away you take yourself with you. And as I discovered, you also bring yourself back again. So I resumed my life as before.

I started by taking a holiday in Florence with a group of dear women friends with whom I had worked in UNISON; we had won an equal pay case against our employer at an Industrial Tribunal in 2001 and had taken a city break together in each of the six years since then in celebration of this triumph. After Florence I went to visit my son in Scotland where he was then living, spent a few days with Marigold and her husband in their caravan in Sussex, another few days with a friend in Wales, a week in Greece on a yoga and meditation course, and took a trip to Paris on Eurostar with my daughter. By the end of May the following year I had also enjoyed a three-week holiday in Dubai and Malaysia with another friend, taken a trip to North Wales to attend my nephew's wedding and been to Cork with my daughter to visit my son who had by then moved to Ireland. I had also spent a few days in Palma, Majorca with my women friends and been back to Spain on a singing course to claim the free holiday I had earned as a volunteer.

Despite all this activity I still felt the need to do something more meaningful. I was enjoying myself but I was still experiencing the same kind of emptiness and yearning for more fulfilment that I had felt prior to my sojourn in Spain. There was still a yawning gap in my life. I longed to make some sort of contribution to society. I still possessed all the talents and skills which had enabled me to carry out my job as a Regional Women's Officer and I wanted to use them. I needed to feel the sense of satisfaction from a job well done that I had previously felt when I was employed.

I had already toyed with the idea of becoming a magistrate. This I thought would fulfil my need to feel useful. Before making any kind of formal application I decided to find out more about it and had gone along to Reading Magistrates' Court one morning to get an idea of what took place and to see whether I felt I would fit in. I sat in the public seats at the back to watch the proceedings. Before the start of the session a young woman came and sat beside me and started to talk to me. She was waiting for her turn to be called and told me the whole sad story of her predicament. She was poor, unable to pay her debts, had taken some items from a shop without paying and been caught red-handed. She was afraid, unable to cope and needed a shoulder to cry on. When it was her turn to stand in the dock she went up and attempted to plead her case on her own behalf without the help of a lawyer. She had no-one to represent her and was woefully inadequate at the task. She was duly fined by the woman magistrate. Coming down from the dock she quickened her pace towards me and threw herself into my arms and cried. I knew then that I could never do that job. I had always been on the side of the underdog and my sympathies would always be on that side. I would always want to plead on behalf of the person in the dock and I could never be the person doing the condemning.

So there I was in May 2008, over a year since returning from Spain, still feeling a sense of purposelessness and not knowing what to do about it. But I still had the travel bug. The idea of going to Cuba had been floating around at the back of my mind for some months. That country was beginning to change since Fidel Castro had stepped down through illness and his brother Raul had taken over as president two years previously; now was the time to visit before too many changes were made to this communist state. Romantic images of Ché Guevara, classic American cars from the 1950s, the legacy of Ernest Hemingway whose books I had loved in my youth and above all the salsa dancing, were at the forefront of my mind. Looking through my ever-plentiful supply of holiday brochures I found a tour of Cuba which seemed to fit the bill. It would start in the southern end of the island at Holguin and would take two weeks to travel by coach through lots of interesting towns and villages up to Havana at the northern end. The tour company was Saga and I had never travelled with them before. Although I knew that anyone over the age of fifty was eligible for a Saga holiday (and I was now aged sixty-four) for me it still had the image of an old people's holiday and I had until then resisted the idea! However it looked like a well-arranged tour and it was also a holiday designated for single people only which appealed to me as I didn't like the idea of going away with a group of people who were all in couples. There was a date available at the end of June; I was very tempted but I held back from actually booking it.

At about the same time an idea was beginning to take shape in my mind that I could possibly be useful as a volunteer at the Citizens' Advice Bureau. I made an application and was called for interview in Reading. There were two vacancies; one was for the regular job of giving assistance to people who came through the door seeking advice and help with issues such as employment, housing, welfare benefits and debt. The other was a new post for a scheme which was being piloted in a few areas and Reading was one of them. It involved more of a counselling role and was in the field of health education. The successful applicant would be based in various outreach centres where over the course of a few weeks they would see regular clients who were seeking specific support in various matters relating to their health. A course of training in the Bureau's coaching methods would be provided and a commitment to be available for two or three days a week, following an initial training period of ten weeks, was required. This second job was very appealing to me and my interview went well. With my background of training in NLP coaching techniques I felt I would enjoy this role and the interviewers seemed to agree that my skills in this area would be useful. There were two courses of training available, one due to start in June and the other in October. I told them that I was thinking of booking a holiday to Cuba in June and if I were successful I would prefer to start in October. I left the interview feeling very optimistic about this possible new opportunity to do something new and different which would be fulfilling for me and would enable me to make a useful contribution to society.

    I came out of the CAB Office and went straight into the John Lewis department store next door where I bought a casual holiday dress which would be just right for the warm weather in Cuba. I went home and booked the holiday. A few days later I received an email telling me that I had been accepted for the training as a Health Adviser and I was delighted. I replied to the effect that I was now booked to go to Cuba at the end of June and therefore I would be available for the second training course in October. All was arranged; I would have my holiday in Cuba and then I would start working as a volunteer for the CAB. I knew that my future holidays would have to be less frequent because of the time commitment involved and I was prepared to give that commitment.

    On Saturday June 28th I set off for my Cuban adventure. As always with something new I was a little apprehensive but feeling the fear had now become second nature to me. Moreover, since undergoing my Louise Hay teacher training I knew how to love myself so I had paid for an upgrade on my flight; I was going to travel business class. The journey would be nearly ten hours long and I wanted to be comfortable. I had not travelled in business class since the flight home from Thailand with my broken ankle. This would be a lot more comfortable! I felt exhilarated as I arrived at Gatwick, stepping out of the chauffeur-driven car which had collected me from home and taken me to the airport (this was provided as part of the holiday) and walking past the economy class check-in desk towards the separate check-in desk for business class passengers. "How did you reconcile this with your socialist principles?" I was asked many times on that holiday as people got to know me. I saw no contradiction. It was just part of me loving myself. There was only one other person in the tour group who had also booked an upgrade; ironically she was a Tory councillor and she later referred to me as a "Champagne Socialist"!

Because of a very much delayed take-off from Gatwick the pilot decided not to bother landing at Holguin on the southern end of the island where we were due to board a coach to our hotel. Instead, without informing any of the passengers, he carried on flying to Havana at the northern end! Since Cuba is a very large island this meant we had to wait at Havana airport for some hours in the middle of the night until a plane was found to take us back to the southern end where we should have landed. After a very bumpy flight on a very ancient Russian plane and a further bumpy ride in a coach over potholed roads we arrived at our hotel at 5.00am, at least nine hours later than expected. I was exhausted, fed up and angry. This wasn't the kind of adventure I had planned.

The next two weeks however more than made up for my initial disappointment. I had a wonderful time. I steeped myself in Cuban history and wallowed in the ubiquitous presence of posters of Ernesto (Ché) Guevara. I marvelled at the 1950s Chevrolets and other vintage American cars, explored the haunts of Ernest Hemingway and salsa-ed my way through the various "*casas de la trova*" from Santiago de Cuba up to the Tropicana Club in Havana. The holiday exceeded my expectations. There was an extra reason for this. On the second day I was chatting with a few members of the group as we toured a co-operative farm. They were a friendly bunch of people and easy to talk to. That was the first time I remember noticing Martyn but to me he was just another member of the group. That evening a few of us went to the disco in the hotel where some young people were celebrating a birthday and they applauded us for joining in the dancing! Over the next few days Martyn and I would coincidentally find ourselves sitting together at dinner or next to each other on the coach and we began to get to know each other a little better. (Martyn did admit to me later that he had engineered some of these "coincidences".) We found we got on well together and enjoyed each other's company. He was a widower and just a year older than me. On a free day towards the end of the holiday we left the organised group tour, took a taxi into Havana and spent the day there on our own. We even danced together on the floor of the famous Tropicana night club! I was having a holiday romance and I was enjoying it.

**With Martyn in Cuba
July 2008**

At the end of the holiday Martyn bought himself an upgrade for the flight home so that we could fly back together in Business Class. We said goodbye at Gatwick and he asked if he could ring me the next evening. I said yes, and although a little resistant at first, I also agreed to meet up again in a couple of weeks' time. He lived in Devon, some distance from Reading, so we agreed he would come up to spend a couple of days at my home. I had not expected such an outcome to my Cuban adventure. A holiday romance was one thing but this was turning out to be something more enduring.

Soon after returning from Cuba it became apparent that Martyn and I would be visiting each other's homes on a regular basis. Consequently (and rather reluctantly) I phoned the CAB office in Reading to explain that my holiday to Cuba had produced a rather unexpected outcome; I would be unable to make the commitment to give them time on a regular basis as I would be spending a lot of time away from Reading. I would therefore be unable to accept the place on the training course that I had been offered. They said they were disappointed but wished me well and told me I would be welcome to join one of the training courses in the future if I stayed in one place for any length of time.

Once again the direction of my life had taken an unexpected turn, reminding me that nothing stays the same for long and that our plans, once made, are often interrupted. Despite my initial resistance as I fiercely tried to guard the precious independence I had been nourishing for the past twenty-one years, I was finding that I enjoyed being in this relationship. It was a new experience to have one other special person in my life, someone who cared about the ordinary everyday things that I was doing and with whom I could share both the joyful and sad things in my life. I had been in three relationships since getting divorced, with the soldier, the parliamentary agent and the gardener, each of which had lasted between two and four years; I had learned something from each of them and had not repeated the mistakes of my marriage. However, I had not been in a relationship since 1999 and it was now 2008 so this felt very unusual. At the age of sixty-four I had met a very kind, gentle and caring man who was fun to be with, who loved me and wanted to be with me. I was falling in love and feeling like a teenager! The Beatles' song "When I'm Sixty-Four" seemed ironically appropriate!

Martyn and I shared a passion for travelling to different parts of the world and during the next four years we spent holidays together in Tenerife, Lanzarote, Tuscany, Santorini, Spain, Sharm-el-Sheik, the Baltic States, Sicily, Germany, Portugal, Mexico, China, Croatia, Marrakech and India. Perhaps I was subconsciously doing what my mother had urged me to do in her final letter to me and Sally: *"Have as happy an old age as I have had – lots of holidays!"*

Because Martyn's home and mine were so far apart (one hundred and seventy-two miles to be precise) we spent much of the intervening periods between our holidays at each other's homes, his in a village in North Devon and mine in Reading. Thus it was that I became very familiar with the route down which I had travelled to Croyde Bay seven years previously when convalescing after my ankle injury. Echoing the TV slogan I had seen from my hospital bed in Thailand:

"It's amazing what a visit to Cuba can do for life!"

Chapter 24
The path of change continues

"Nothing endures but change."
Heraclitus

"Who am I?", says Jean Valjean in "Les Miserables" as he reflects on his life. After so many changes during my own life's journey I too wonder about my identity. Am I really that same person whose birth was so movingly celebrated in poetry by her father and who, along with her sister, was so cherished in childhood by her mother? Am I really that same person who in the "swinging sixties" travelled across Europe in a London double-decker bus and who actually met the Beatles? Am I really that same woman whose life in the 1970s revolved around bringing up her two children, teaching a class of thirty others and trying to maintain a sense of normality whilst living with a man who kept the household in fear? Am I really that same woman who in the 1980s managed to break through that fear to find freedom from that man's tyranny? Am I really that same woman who in the 1990s actually stood for Parliament and went on pursuing the quest to become an MP until all hope was lost? Am I really that same person who in the first decade of the twenty-first century went on to make a journey into her inner self which was much more difficult and meaningful than any previous outward achievement? And am I even now, in the second decade of this new millennium, still continuing to change and to learn? Has the whole process thus far been a laborious but fascinating way of finding out that the only true purpose in life is simply to be? Perhaps it has. Maybe each person is after all simply a collection of their own stories; the philosopher David Hume has described this as "the bundle theory of self".

In the early hours of Wednesday May 19th, 2010 my dear friend Marigold died. She had been diagnosed with ovarian cancer four years previously so we knew it was coming. But it was still a shock. I watched her enjoy those last few years to the full and then saw her slowly fade. During those four years she made sure she had all the experiences she wanted. I admired her determination to seize every moment. She enjoyed some marvellous holidays abroad with her husband Rod and saw places in this country that she had always wanted to visit, as well as Iona in Scotland. She and I ate some wonderful lunches in good restaurants in and around Berkshire and Oxfordshire and we went to see lots of London shows together, including "Calendar Girls", "The History Boys" and a performance by the Cirque du Soleil at the Royal Albert Hall. The two of us even enjoyed a champagne afternoon tea at Claridge's as part of her seventieth birthday celebrations in 2009. As I sat there in the elegant dining room, eating my finger sandwiches and strawberry pastries off fine china plates, the irony of my having marched past the Ritz all those years ago singing "Burn it down" did not escape me!

It was only in the last few months of her life that Marigold had to curtail her activities through lack of energy. Despite this, only two months before she died she managed to give a magnificent party to celebrate her Golden Wedding, where she and Rod were dancing until midnight! Marigold was such a free spirit and I loved her for it. It was in the weeks following that wonderful celebration that she would phone me around 4.00am telling me that she was scared. All I could do was to listen. Visiting her in the hospice during those last few weeks was extremely painful. I had never seen anyone approaching their certain death and I found it inconceivable that soon she would not exist anymore. I still find it incomprehensible that she is no longer here. She was my closest friend and now she is gone.

Marigold was the only person of my own generation whose death I have encountered. The death of my father was a fact I had grown up with since babyhood: it just seemed "normal" to me as I had known nothing else. The sudden and tragic way in which my mother died was a devastating shock but her death was nevertheless something I knew I would have had to face in the future, albeit probably more gradually and with some preparation. But to have my friend die, someone only four years older than me, was a new and shocking experience and it brought home to me in a new way the transience of life and the reality of my own mortality. Once again Andrew Marvell's words rang in my ears:

> "But at my back I always hear
> Time's winged chariot hurrying near."

I was on a week's holiday in Sharm-el-Sheik with Martyn when some of those night-time phone calls from Marigold took place and just a few days before her death I was on a city break to Istanbul with my women friends. There I was, still actively enjoying my life, making the most of my good health and good fortune and my friend was in the throes of death. I am glad that I was able to return in time to bid her farewell. She had come to the end of all her Fridays and I would continue to live the rest of mine without her.

Chapter 25

A final message from my father

"Freedom is the sure possession of those alone who have the courage to defend it."
Pericles
(Inscribed at the base of the Bomber Command Memorial Sculpture)

2012 was the year in which the Mayan prophecy was widely discussed in the Western world. There had been many different interpretations of the meaning of the end of the thirteenth Baktun in the Mayan calendar. Some had imagined it to foretell the end of the world; others had seen it as bringing in a shift in human consciousness throughout our planet. As the date of December 21st approached, which happened to fall on a Friday, I was one of those who chose to approach it with a sense of hope and optimism.

During my trip to Mexico with Martyn two years previously our tour guide had provided an explanation of some of the intricacies of the Mayan calendar while we toured the various ancient sites on the Yucatan peninsula. I remember particularly our early morning visit to the jungle to see the ruins of the lost Mayan city of Palenque. As we stood in the mist below the huge Temple of the Inscriptions, which houses the tomb of the ruler Pacal the Great, we learned about the end-of-the-world predictions and Western misinterpretations of the meaning of the Mayan calendar.

The Mayans believed that the Universe is destroyed and then recreated at the start of each Universal cycle. As each Baktun comes to an end another one begins. Hearing this had been enough to dispel for me any possible thoughts of doom and gloom as that significant Friday drew nearer. Like each Baktun, as one year comes to an end another year begins and as one week comes to an end another week begins. However, there was a much more personal way in which that year held significance for me, and it came about in a way that I could never have imagined.

On Thursday June 28th, a Memorial to all the 55,573 aircrew of Bomber Command who lost their lives in the Second World War was dedicated and unveiled in Green Park, London by Her Majesty the Queen. As the next of kin to one of those 55,573 men, I was privileged to receive an invitation be present at that ceremony and Martyn accompanied me. It took place the day after what would have been my father's ninety-third birthday. There were many men present on that day who were around that age. As a Lancaster Bomber dropped poppies over the crowds on that hot summer's day I was deeply moved. For me this was the funeral my father had never had. I was proud to wear his medal, the DFC and bar, which had been presented to my mother by King George V1 sixty-six years previously on Tuesday April 9th, 1946.

**At the Bomber Command Memorial Sculpture
June 28th 2012**

One month after attending the Memorial Dedication Ceremony I received a further intervention in my life concerning my father. It brought me by far the most incredible piece of information yet. I had received a phone call from a genealogist in 1997 bringing me news of unknown cousins on my father's side; I had received a letter in 2002 from a man in the Czech Republic thanking me for the bombing mission my father had carried out on the German oil industry; I was now about to learn the most amazing news of all. Once again it came to me by a very circuitous route.

In April 2012 I had joined Facebook. I had resisted it until then, considering it more suitable for young people rather than those in their late sixties. However, Martyn's daughter Clare had recently set up a Facebook page to advertise her bakery business and I wanted to send her my congratulations so I joined Facebook. In July Clare told us that she had received a mysterious comment on her Facebook page from a Canadian called Fraser Muir who said he was trying to contact me and my sister Sally in connection with our father. He had been looking for us on Facebook, had noticed that the bakery business was on the list of my Facebook "friends" and as there hadn't been much activity on my own Facebook page he had posted a message on Clare's page instead.

I told Sally about this just before Martyn and I went away for a weekend in Kent to attend the naming ceremony for Clare's youngest daughter. As we were driving back to Reading after the event I received a text from Sally saying she had just read a Facebook message from Fraser Muir. In it he revealed that he had been on the same bombing mission as the one on which our father was killed and even more astonishingly he had actually heard the last words our father had spoken! Sally had read those words and told me she was in tears. I could hardly wait to get home to read it all for myself. I too was in tears as I read the following message from Fraser Muir on Facebook:

"I'm so pleased to finally make contact with you and your family as I feel I somehow have a bond with you as your Dad is a major part of what I remember about my tour of thirty-five operations.

I had wondered many times about what it would be like to be hit by flak and what reaction one would take. Well I remember the night over Böhlen, your Dad was directing the operation, and I remember him being in complete control, when he calmly announced "Oh Damn, I've been hit. I'm going down. Number two take over, number two take over". Then number two came in, then another voice jumped in and claimed he was number two. Then all hell broke out and it ended in a real shouting match and the operation was a failure.

For years I often wondered if in fact your father made it, and about two or three years ago I went to a meeting of the Air Crew Association in Toronto and there was a book sale being held prior to the meeting and I bought a copy of "Bomber Command War Diaries", and it was there that I found out that he was buried in the Berlin War Cemetery. I was so disappointed as I had prayed for years that someday I would get to meet him. I have contacted the head of the Bomber Command Association and told him about how cool your Dad was and my comments have been recorded in the History of Bomber Command.

The other fact that your Dad and I have in common is that we have the same birthday, June 27th. I was five years younger. Too bad we weren't able to meet at the unveiling."

Once again my father had come back to speak to me. The very last words he had spoken were now being relayed to me sixty-seven years later. What had happened on the night of February 19th/20th 1945 had never been fully understood by my mother or the authorities. I had read letters from RAF officials, family, friends and colleagues, letters that my mother had kept all her life, but most of them were just conjecture as to what might have happened. The bare facts were that my father's plane had been shot down, that it was unlikely that he had been taken prisoner and more likely that he had been killed outright. I had no real conception of what had actually occurred. I had no idea that my father had said anything in those last moments of his life and now I was being told not only that he had indeed spoken, but also what those words were, and most incredibly of all that there was someone alive in the world today who had heard those words, who still remembered them and who had been affected by them all his life!

This was almost too much to take in. For our benefit Fraser Muir then wrote a fuller account of his story on a website called Aircrew Association. He calls it his "Once in a million moment":

Looking back on my tour of thirty-five bombing operations I have many memorable and raw moments, but the chances of this one happening, I suggest, is "one in a million".

This story began back on a bombing operation on Böhlen, near Leipzig; our target was an oil refinery. I had often wondered what it would be like in an aircraft once it had been damaged by a "German Night Fighter" or hit by flak; how would the crew react with the realization they were going down?

At the time my crew were nearing the end of our "Tour of Operations", and we could have been classified as a "Seasoned Crew", but nothing could prepare me for what happened that night.

When we arrived over the target, the Master Bomber was in complete control, I remember his clear commands to the Pathfinders directing them to drop their various colored flares in their role of "marking the target". Then the Master Bomber calmly announced in the clearest, coolest voice imaginable, "Oh Damn, I've been hit. I'm going down. Number two take over, number two take over". A voice came on stating he was Number two, followed by a second voice claiming he was number two ....then all hell broke loose with a lot of yelling and clear chaos. Not surprisingly, the operation was abandoned, and later classified as being unsuccessful. What amazed me though, was the voice of the Master Bomber; there was no panic, no shouting, he seemed to be more concerned with his responsibility of passing on his command to Number two, than the fact he was on his way down. It was the calm, collected, controlled nature of his voice that has made it one of the most vivid memories of my tour of thirty-five bombing operations.

Over the years I have often thought of this Master Bomber and whether he may have survived that frightful night. There was always the hope that he may have. By chance a couple of years ago at a meeting of the Ontario Air Crew Association there was a book sale being held prior to the meeting. I stumbled upon and purchased a copy of "The Bomber Command War Diaries". It was through this publication that I was able to identify the Master Bomber as Wing Commander E. A. Benjamin, D.F.C. and Bar, and that he is buried in the Berlin War Cemetery. To say I am saddened to learn that he had died is an understatement. At every Mass I have attended over the years, (and I have attended many!), I have included him in my prayers said with those for my fallen comrades. Each time, I hoped that he may well have gone down but survived the hit.

Now this is not the end of my story... following our return from the recent unveiling of the Bomber Command memorial in London, England, I visited the website and began reading the comments. Imagine my surprise when I came across one written by a Jeannie Benjamin who had attended the unveiling of the memorial in respect of her father Wing Commander Eric A. Benjamin! I was thrilled. I immediately checked Facebook, and sure enough her page appeared. I sent her a message, but after a week or so with no reply and recognizing there was not a great deal of activity on her Facebook wall, I decided to check her friends that were listed. It was then I found her sister, Sally. I sent her a message, and within a few days I received a reply that she and her sister were gobsmacked to receive my message. They asked me to tell them more and so I promised to write out this story that I have carried over all these years describing what I remember when their Dad and I were both in the skies over Böhlen on the night of February 19/20, 1945.

Jeannie and Sally were just wee ones at the time of their father's tragic death; Jeannie, a toddler of eighteen months and Sally, only three weeks old. They are overjoyed in finding me, one person who remembers hearing the last words spoken by their Dad, and I am ecstatic in finding "my Master Bomber's" family to share my indirect, but profound experience with those who love him the most. I've agreed to try to answer any question they might have about this time in history...a silver lining in a very dark ominous cloudy sky.

Another interesting connection that I have with W/C Benjamin is that we both share the same birthday.... June 27th. At the time of the bombing over Böhlen he was twenty-five and I was twenty. May he rest in peace eternally.

Fraser A. Muir
August 14, 2012

If only I had been able to meet this man on the day of the unveiling of the Bomber Command Memorial. Fraser Muir had travelled from Canada especially to attend this long-awaited event and had been present in the same invited audience as me and yet neither of us knew of the other's existence. This man, who had had such a direct connection with my father and who has told me in a recent email that he feels he shares being part of my family, was there in the crowd as the poppies floated down out of the sky. How close to him I was I will never know. Perhaps the day will still come when we may meet; I could yet decide to take another trip to Canada and come face to face with the man who heard the last words my father ever spoke.

Afterword

"Our own life has to be our message."
Thich Nhat Hanh

It was the renewed realisation that nothing lasts forever which gave me the final push to write this book. I first had the idea and even the title in 2002, when my daughter reminded me of the kitchen table conversation which had taken place in the house in Dartford Road, Sevenoaks all those years earlier but I didn't actually start the process of writing until 2006, the year that Marigold was diagnosed with ovarian cancer. Even then I wrote only spasmodically and in longhand until a few weeks before she died, when I began in earnest on my computer. She became my inspiration and I hope she knew it.

I am still living in the home in Reading which I bought twenty years ago (and which I imagined I would occupy for only a couple of years before finding a safe Parliamentary seat and moving north!) and I become ever more conscious of the folly of living life in the future at the expense of the now. I have recently had some improvements made to the fabric of my house - work which could have been carried out long ago but which I resisted for many years, telling myself that it wasn't worth doing as I would soon be moving on. I am now enjoying the fruits of those improvements, recognising that although I may make plans for the future it is now that matters. I do still have many plans, hopes and wishes, not all of which will be within my control, but as each of my Fridays comes and goes, along with the attendant changes in between, I do my best to heed the wise words of the serenity prayer, so often attributed to Saint Augustine or Thomas Aquinas, but perhaps more authentically owed to Reinhold Neibuhr:

"God, grant me the serenity to accept
The things I cannot change,
Courage to change the things I can,
And the wisdom to know the difference."

If I can get even a glimpse of that wisdom then I am optimistic for all the Fridays yet to come.

A Postscript

The Universe continues to deliver up delightful little surprises for me. After completing this book I gave a party to celebrate my seventieth birthday on Saturday August 17th, 2013 and I hired an Abba tribute group. Martyn and I had become big fans of Abba after seeing the show "Mamma Mia" soon after we returned from Cuba. Since then we have danced to the songs of Abba in countries all over the world!

Continuing this theme we took a holiday together in May 2014 on the Greek Island of Skiathos where we enjoyed a wonderful boat trip visiting all the beaches made famous by the film of "Mamma Mia". Adjacent to our hotel was a small church. It was dedicated to a saint who had been given the name of the day on which she was born. The church was called Agia Paraskevi, which translates as Saint Friday!

Outside the Church of Agia Paraskevi
Friday May 23rd 2014

ABOUT THE AUTHOR

Jeannie Benjamin spent the first twenty-one years of her working life as a primary school teacher. She became interested in politics and stood for Parliament in the 1992 General Election as the Labour Candidate in Sevenoaks. She then began working for the trade union UNISON, focusing on women's development and training. She moved into the field of personal coaching and qualified as a Louise Hay teacher and NLP Master Practitioner.

She travels abroad several times a year and when she is in England she enjoys living in her home in Reading and making frequent visits to North Devon. She has two adult children, a son and a daughter.

Printed in Great Britain
by Amazon.co.uk, Ltd.,
Marston Gate.